# Guardians of Mediocrity:

## How Universities Use Tenure Denial to Thwart Change, Creativity, and Intellectual Innovation

Copyright © 2017 of collected work belongs to Foiled Crown Books, LLC
Copyright © 2017 of each individual essay belongs to its respective creator and is reproduced here with permission.

All rights reserved. No part of this book may be reproduced in any form by any electronic or mechanical means including photocopying, recording, or information storage and retrieval without permission in writing for the copyright holder(s).

In most cases, the identity of individuals and institutions in these essays has been redrawn, made into composites, and/or obscured with pseudonyms so as to afford protection. The publisher makes no claims as to the veracity of any statements made by the authors in this collection.

The following essay originally appeared in an online literary journal and is reprinted here with permission from the journal's editorial board:

    McElmurray, Karen Salyer. "Outside the Outside." *Drafthorse*, winter 2014.

Cover and Book Design: Madeline Grey

ISBN: 978-1-944355-01-2

Foiled Crown Books
Newburgh, NY 12550
https://foiledcrownbooks.com
Email: editor@foiledcrownbooks.com

Printed in U.S.A

# Guardians of Mediocrity:

## How Universities Use Tenure Denial to Thwart Change, Creativity, and Intellectual Innovation

Foiled Crown Books, LLC

# CONTENTS

Preface

Ashes Gone Cold: Academic Life and Death on the Tenure Line   13
*Ed Rafferty*

She Who Is Looking Her Age   27
*J.W. Young*

The Mean Girls' Club at Red County Community College   39
*Madeline Grey*

The Thing With Feathers:
My Five Years at a Small Church College   53
*Nancy McCabe*

Crossing the Bridge: My Long Road to Tenure   69
*Robert E Brown*

Stop Clock, Cover Mirror   83
*Kathleen Davies*

Arbitrary & Capricious   101
*Michaela Valentine*

Academic Slavery At A Prestigious Cancer Center   107
*Kapil Mehta and Reeta Mehta*

Outside The Outside   115
*Karen Salyer McElmurray*

Why I Quit My Teaching Career in Texas
and Why I Understand If You Do the Same   125
*Duana Welch*

**About the Authors**

**Further Reading**

# Preface

*It really is necessary for us to "break the silence" about tenure denial in order fully to face its consequences.*
—Charles Stivale, "Tenure and Its Denial"

The essays in this collection document abuses of power with regard to tenure reviews on college and university campuses in the United States. We received interest from numerous would-be participants who, for many similar reasons—lingering stress from the hostile climate associated with their tenure denial or ongoing court cases—could not complete their stories, or who did not want to risk going public for fear of reprisal or of damaging their career prospects. One of the first communications we received in response to our call for papers was from a man who had served on a tenure committee who berated us and told us that we were "arrogant and needed to let it go." He falsely assumed that this call had come from the junior faculty whose tenure he had helped deny and who, he said, was "complaining about it all over the *Chronicle*." This first contact only seemed to prove the validity of the project in terms of why we set out to offer this space so that those who had been denied tenure could tell their stories.

Based on the responses we received from interested contributors, we can conclude that a preponderance of the college teachers being unfairly denied tenure are from humanities disciplines. The majority of them are also women and their cases involve, inevitably, some degree of sexual harassment or ideologically gendered attack. What we've compiled here does not attempt to reflect those statistics. Instead, we sought to collect as varied a group of stories as possible, including two final essays not by professors who were denied tenure but by faculty who left their positions voluntarily (Karen Salyer McElmurray even left a tenured professorship) due to the same abusive dynamics that have resulted in unjust tenure decisions. We included these last two essays as a way to broaden the discussion—the issue here does not only pertain to institutional failures to check the power of incompetent and malicious administrators; it is also about the nature of higher education, about our values as a country at this particular time in history, about the anti-intellectual forces that prevail in discussions of civil rights and equality.

The intrepid authors who have offered their stories for inclusion in this collection represent a small percentage of the large (and growing) body of teacher-scholars with advanced degrees who are surviving a denial of tenure. We believe this points to a dire need to revise the tenure application process.

We hope that if you are in that group of survivors, that you will find comfort in these stories. You are not alone. Many others have lived through the same situation and gone on to successful positions in academia and elsewhere. We hope you take heart from the fact that all of the authors in this collection who were once denied tenure are currently thriving. Many of us still do not understand what really happened to cause our tenure denial, as so often private conversations between toxic personalities fueled such decisions and those cannot be viewed in an employment file. Chances are that most of us will never know what really happened behind closed doors. Those who are lucky to have documentation and an effective Union are usually the ones who win lawsuits.

If you are a junior faculty or graduate student reading this collection in order to get a sense of what you should do (or not do) in order to eventually receive tenure at an academic institution, the first advice we might give you is to thoroughly investigate the policies, procedures, and politics of any institution that makes you a job offer. Make sure that they abide by the AAUP's recommendation for clarity, consistency, and candor in the tenure application process. We understand that the academic job market is extremely competitive these days, but many of the authors who have been denied tenure would admit that the initial mistake was accepting a job offer from an institution that was not a good fit for their professional goals or ideological values. Many would suggest that it is better to turn down a job offer than take one that might eventually lead to a tenure denial.

But these days, a tenure denial is not the "kiss of death" it used to be. Being denied tenure does not necessarily kill your academic career, just as the increased prevalence of insoluble home mortgages in the real estate collapse of a few years ago has meant that people who foreclosed on a home are moving on after just a couple of years to purchase another one. The more common the occurrence, the less damaging it is—and, unfortunately, tenure denials are increasing in their frequency. Some attribute this to the university's growing reliance on adjunct faculty. Predatory administrators view adjuncts as preferable to tenure-track faculty because they do not have to pay them as much, they do not have to offer them benefits, and they are easy to control since they are only given semester-by-semester work. Adjuncts are very rarely unionized. They have little freedom and little protection.

Once you are hired in a tenure-track position, make sure to seek out the assistance of a trusted mentor at your school who can help you navigate through the vast (and seemingly ever growing) bureaucracy that now oversees faculty retention and promotion. Making good friends among the faculty in your department will help your chances of getting tenure; alternatively, it will help your chances of getting a job elsewhere should you be denied. You will want to have letters of recommendation from people at that institution who can speak to your good work.

By the beginning of 2017, lawmakers in at least three states have proposed bills that would do away with the university tenure system entirely. It's likely that all of the authors published in this collection would agree: if the college and university tenure system were to be abolished, faculty would be at an even higher risk for pernicious and arbitrary treatment by a group of political elite who are often anti-woman, anti-homosexual, and anti-minority. The protections afforded by tenure are necessary in order to make changes to a dysfunctional system that is minimizing the idea of shared governance and giving in to a top-down hierarchy of power that is not conducive to equality or fairness. It's important to understand that employees of public colleges and universities are employees of the state: their employment terms are bound up in Constitutional law, meaning that while private companies (or private colleges) can fire employees "at will," the Constitution guarantees that governmental institutions cannot infringe on citizens' free speech, such as through the termination of a teaching position because of the nature of the faculty's research. As these essays show, foxes are in charge of the hen house, and they cannot be trusted to play fairly of their own accord. We need a revision of tenure procedures, not abolition.

To put it bluntly: this book is not intended to be used as evidence that we should do away with the tenure system. If you read the stories here and believe that tenure is not a valid institution, then you have missed the point entirely. The faculty telling their stories here are speaking out against injustices because they care about the quality of our country's educational institutions; they care about making them better. Tenure is not perfect, but it has never been and will never be some kind of "job for life" authorization that inflates student tuition. As Professor William Van Alstyne explains in an AAUP Bulletin from 1971:

> Tenure, accurately and unequivocally defined, lays no claim whatever to a guarantee of lifetime employment. Rather, *tenure provides only that no person continuously retained as a full-time faculty member beyond a specified lengthy period of probationary service may thereafter be dismissed without adequate cause.* . . . [T]enure is translatable as a statement of formal assurance that. . . the individual's professional security and academic freedom will not be placed in question without the observance of *full academic due process.*

Tenure is a necessary feature of higher education because in a democracy we care about due process and about protecting freedoms. However, the procedures for achieving tenure need to be re-evaluated at most institutions of higher education. As the events described in these essays attest, we need better checks and balances, better oversight, so that self-serving administrators, incompetent department chairs, and petty senior colleagues cannot take out their personal vendettas against unsuspecting and hard-working junior faculty members. As faculty salaries stagnate and student tuition increases, we need to shrink the top-heavy bureaucratic system that only serves to justify the positions (and increased salaries) of higher-level administrators, a system that consistently fails faculty members and students. We have a long way to go in order to achieve this, and if we are afraid of losing our jobs for speaking out against those in power then these changes can never happen. Moreover, our system of higher education will have ceased to stand on democratic principles.

A denial of tenure does not mean that your life is over, even though it may feel that way at the time. It can be a good opportunity for growth and redirection. It can be the wake-up call that brings you to a happier, more fulfilling life. Now a full professor, Lennard Davis recounts the unexpected positive effects he experienced after his tenure denial:

> I had the rare opportunity of finding out the true nature of love and support from my friends and family. My wife helped me through many dark moments. It was especially hard telling my young children that, essentially, I had been fired. But my fears that they would see their father as a failure were unfounded. Rather, my difficulties gave them a way to understand their own struggles, and my persistence helped them to be feisty in their own lives. ("Beyond Tenure")

Also on the bright side—unemployment services offer many subsidies for new training or for starting your own business, and hefty court settlements can fund your research and travel for many years.

Most of all, we want you to know that if you have been denied tenure, you are not alone—plenty of talented people have experienced this same thing. We assure you that if you were conscientious in your pursuit of the regular standards for retention in your discipline, then this decision wasn't about you at all; it was about the toxic environment on your campus.

Madeline Grey
New Haven, Connecticut
January 2017

# Ashes Gone Cold:
## Academic Life and Death on the Tenure Line

## Ed Rafferty

The Letter (yes, a capital L) arrived at the end of September. Seven years ago. I remember the contents, and I remember reading it on my lawn, before my children came home from school. I do not have it anymore. I threw the damn thing out. By the time it came—as registered mail—I knew the basic contents. Tenure denied (well, sort of; more on that later). But that knowledge did not do much to blunt the effect of reading it. Punch in the gut. Slap in the face. Kick as I was down. Although I knew the news already—the chair of my department had told me a few weeks before—I still thought that maybe it said something else. Stages of grief, I guess. Bargaining, denial, certainly depression had already washed over me again and again. I did not go through these in any logical order or procession. Nope. Just wildly swinging back and forth.

The delay in getting The Letter was part of my process of tenure denial. It was a few weeks between the news from my chair at the beginning of the semester, and the actual arrival of a formal letter from the institution. I had been dealing with hearsay, innuendo, and rumor for months. Let me say here that I was not officially "denied" tenure. At my research institution in the urban northeast, there was a rarely used part of the faculty handbook—in fact, one that is no longer extant—that permitted the Provost to just postpone a tenure decision for three years. No explanation was required. That is what happened to me. The university decided not to decide. But I was also told—more rumor though this came directly from people in the know—that "there was nothing I could do to get tenure." After eight years of graduate school, then adjuncting, then working on the margins of the university, then finally landing a teaching job, publishing, and building a network of colleagues in the profession, my career was over. It was a big "F" on my academic life and my self-identity.

Or, so I thought and felt at the time. My hope is that this essay is more than just naval gazing and catharsis. There is certainly some of that, I am sure, and I beg the reader's indulgence for it. But what I want to offer most is some advice, guidance, even mentorship perhaps. What happens when you are denied tenure? How do we find answers to questions? What do we do with our careers? Where do we turn for advice, for counsel, for help?

We need essays that do this. We need stories that tell us about career changes, stories about depression and fear that is grappled with, and overcome. Academics spend their lives talking and writing and meeting. But not about this topic. I have not seen many (any?) conference proceedings or conference panels dealing with tenure denial. No titles on "The Dynamics of Tenure Denial," or "The History of Tenure Denial," or "The University Hegemon: Tenure Denial and Individual Agency in the Academy." The job registers do not spent time on it, career offices do not offer training in it, and statistics are not widely kept or easily accessible institution by institution. It is only heard and discussed in whispers.

I spent some time reading and researching materials on tenure denial in the last few years. Nothing systematic, mind you, just a perusal of the materials that I turned to for my own guidance, help, and counseling. There is scant material on the subject. There are some occasional articles in the *Chronicle of Higher Education*, some in *Education Week*, or *Inside Higher Education*, and certainly articles in newspapers about high profile cases or cases that go into the court system. There are also a number of blogs and websites—generally associated with a single individual denied tenure—that offer personal narratives, occasional guidance, and links of interest. But tenure denial is not an especially popular topic.

Most of the essays, blogs, and websites are of two basic types. The first essays are just angry screeds. They are actually my favorite to read because they still capture my own anger after several years regarding my tenure process, and they are frankly more realistic. The second are the celebration essays: "I was denied tenure at institution X, and I am now a successful professor at the better institution Y." There are two subtypes of these celebration essays. The first subtype is usually written from rather unknown professors who counsel individuals to keep their chins up, continue to publish, keep networks of colleagues outside the institution that denied you, and just apply to jobs again. With persistence and a little luck—though I have to say it is mostly persistence that is focused on—a job at another institution will come to pass, and you will be the happier for it. The second subtype are the celebrated cases of well-known professors—public intellectuals—who run afoul of their home institution in some way but land on their feet almost immediately at another top tier research institution. This top tier institution does not hesitate to offer tenure. I have nothing in particular against these essays and narratives (though nearly all of them seem to be written by men). It is perfectly fine and well that those individuals succeeded, remained professors, and continued their careers. But they did not offer me much comfort, guidance, or direction.

I take as my title a play on the Thomas Hardy poem "The Dead Man Walking." You feel your "ashes gone cold" when tenure is denied; you are indeed a "dead man walking." You still hang around the institution for a while; but you are there as a ghost:

> *They hail me as one living,*
> *But don't they know*

> *That I have died of late years,*
> *Untombed although?*

So, while the available information and essays offer some hope to the denied, I am more inclined to think about the ways that institutions and professional associations fail to create an atmosphere of openness about tenure, its prospects and also its perils, and the ways that careers can be fashioned in a discipline in multiple ways beyond the tenure line. Since tenure is seemingly on a slow trickling decline—countless articles appear every year about the end of tenure—then graduate education, training, and, yes, career counseling, needs to fit the reality of the actual paths that most of us will experience and pursue while on and off the tenure line.

## LIFE ON THE TENURE LINE

A personal account of my own story is warranted here, I think, to give context to the experience of denial. I worked at a major research institution in the urban northeast. My training is as a historian but I worked in a department that dealt more with the core curriculum and not in a traditional history department; most of us would be called "interdisciplinary." The work was rewarding but demanding. High teaching loads, large lecture classes (we averaged around 110 students per semester), no teaching assistants, little to no ability to really gain significant time off for research and writing before the tenure review. We worked on one-year renewable assistant professor contracts based on enrollment in our program. After a certain number of years, generally five, you could be offered a two-year contract and apply for tenure and promotion. Hence, we had something of a traditional seven-year tenure clock. Getting sabbaticals from the institution was essentially out of the question until tenure was granted. You were on a one-year contract, so you could not get time off because the institution might struggle to fill the vacancy. In addition, there was the added problem of what they did with the recently hired individual at the end of their one-year position. Even getting outside funding was questionable. There was no guarantee that there was a job at the end of your outside funding. Enrollment might change. Why not simply renew the person hired to replace you (after all, you left the institution to write and research; they still had to teach the students that were there). Or, a program or part of a program could be closed or curtailed. A year before my tenure case, the school had curtailed parts of a program and did not renew the contracts of 7 faculty members that had previously taught in that program. They were not "fired" since they were on one-year contracts that were not renewed.

During each year leading up to the tenure application you were essentially working for the Dread Pirate Roberts (from the book and film *The Princess Bride*). "Good night, Ed," I would hear in my head. "Good work.

Sleep well. We'll most likely not renew you in the morning." Maybe, many of us in my position at the university hoped, we too could learn the secrets of the institution and become the Dread Pirate Roberts (i.e. an associate professor with tenure). We might be able to change the system from within, or mentor people through the process in a way that we were not mentored. Or, we too could just deny them in the morning once we had tenure given the constraints of university finances, enrollment, and institutional needs across multiple colleges and departments.

My renewals did keep coming, and I managed to have some successes along the way. My teaching evaluations were generally strong—ranked in the top part of my department. That was important. In fact, each year as renewals came up for discussion, your evaluations were key. The institution graphed you against every other member of the college. You could see what evaluation number you had to hit year to year in order to maintain employment. The graph was interesting since it was on a one to five scale. But in order to show difference between say a 4.1 and a 4.2, the space graphed between was huge. It made you feel deeply inadequate to be at 4.1 when you could see your unnamed colleagues on the graph higher at a 4.2 average, let alone the tenured members who were perhaps pointed out to be at 4.4, 4.5, or a 4.6. They were clearly significantly above your 4.1. But maybe you were better than the math professor who ranked at a lowly 3.9 average. At least, that is what was encouraged in the process. I am not sure why a 3.9 professor is worse than a 4.1 professor and obviously not tenureable compared to a 4.4 professor. But that was the process of contract renewal, merit raises, and promotion.

I had some other successes as well. I published a book. I contributed to my department's work by serving on search committees, managed to get a position on the faculty senate of the university, served on a search committee for a new dean in another college at the institution, served in professional capacities on a national professional association, and served on a regional professional association. I continued to write book reviews for professional publications. I attended conferences and presented papers. I did the whole careerism part of academe although I did not feel much motivated by it and was not terribly good at it. I obtained a second book contract, and started work on that. New conference papers proceeded from that project. My teaching was good, my service was good, and my publishing seemed pretty good. I think that I was on a solid track, and my departmental evaluations each year were solid. The department did not mention anything to me to worry about.

But not everything was rosy. No failed tenure cases really ever can be. I fell behind on the second book project. I had children (four in total). My wife had a career. I had all the pressures everyone else dealt with at this point in their lives. I also had no mentorship, no one telling me that I was not on pace for tenure, or that I should forgo family time or service time or teaching time to apply for tenure. I was on my own, and since my evaluations were strong I thought I was still fine. This is one factor in many tenure cases. Mentoring within the institution should be an aspect of every college; and, it should happen not just within a department alone because there can be fault lines in departments, personal grievances, axes to grind, that will sink any application before the candidate can even figure out what happened or where they went wrong.

In December 2007, my department and college asked whether I might want to go up for tenure early. My case was strong, the department thought, and since "changes were coming to the college and university," it might be good to get the tenure case going right away. I agreed, and wrote to the Provost in January 2008 requesting an early tenure review for the following academic year starting in June 2008.

So began the process. In early summer, I submitted my application to the department and waited. The department approved the application unanimously by the beginning of the academic year. The college tenure and promotion committee also approved the application unanimously that fall. The dean of the college approved the recommendation of the department and the college, and sent the application to the university tenure and promotion committee. In late December, a member of the committee—and a senior faculty member in my college—called my office, and said "This conversation is not official. But you have nothing to worry about. The committee approved the application." And so, I finished the fall semester pleased that I had survived the process. Hurrah, tenure had been granted.

Through the second semester, I awaited official word of the committee's decision, which from previous experience generally occurred in February. But word never came. In March 2009, the Provost requested that I provide extra materials for review. I was never told why extra materials were necessary. I had thought that the application had been closed. At least, that is what the department told me when I finished the application in June. I complied, adding parts of my second working manuscript (less than I would have liked), an additional book review that appeared after my summer submission, and a copy of a newsletter that I edited for a professional association in my field.

And I waited. No word about my case came from the Provost office in April, May, June, July, or August. It was now 19 months since I had requested an early tenure review. It was 14 months since I finished my application. In late August, the university again requested more materials to add to my tenure file for review. A phone call came while I was on vacation with my family, and the university asked "how much more have you written since June?" I did not really have much to add, and asked whether this is how the tenure process typically worked. Was a case kept open for review at the university level to see what the candidate would do as the process unfolded? I did not add to the tenure file that August. I had already suspected that something was wrong, and had heard through the grapevine that no tenure decisions had been made for that year. I began to think that I had to find another job. After all, my contract was set to expire, the university had made no decision in my tenure case, and I needed a job.

I met with my Chair when the school year started in September, and finally heard directly from him that tenure was not going to be granted. That is when I waited for The Letter.

### CAREER DEATH ON THE TENURE LINE

> *Not at a minute's warning,*
>     *Not in a loud hour,*
> *For me ceased Time's enchantments*
>     *In hall and bower.*
>
> *There was no tragic transit,*
>     *No catch of breath,*
> *When silent seasons inched me*
>     *On to this death...*

—excerpt from Thomas Hardy "The Dead Man Walking"

The Letter noted that my case was to be postponed, and that I could reapply for tenure at the end of the new probationary period in three years. The materials most relevant to this new review, the Letter said, would be what I had done since the new probationary period began; what I had done for the first review was less important in the process. I was to be subject to whatever new rules were in place for tenure review at the new review year. The university was in the midst of shifting aspects of the tenure process so I knew that new rules were to be forthcoming. Finally, none of the outside reviewers of my first application for tenure—there were 11 outside letters for the process—could be reviewers for my second application for tenure (when the number of reviewers was to increase). The Letter said I should read the committee's report carefully to see where I could improve. But since the committee report indicated that they approved me for tenure and promotion, I was not sure what I should do based on that report. There was to be no contact with the Provost about the decision. Any discussions of tenure were to go back to my department since the process was to start over again. The only indication in the report was a single line that said my publication record (a book, an article, a few book reviews, editorial work, conference papers, and a second book under contract) was a little lower than members of the History department. But I was not in the History department at the university, and had never met with the chair of that department to discuss tenure. Should I meet with them to discuss my progress, I wondered? I actually thought my progress was roughly similar to assistant professors in that department but perhaps it was not.

In any case, I was told privately that tenure was not going to be granted no matter what I did. Now what? Well, the college offered that I could take a renewable multiyear contract and no longer be eligible for tenure if that is something that I wanted to do. In fact, this was the change that happened at the university as I made my tenure application. We were no longer offering renewable one-year assistant professor contracts but instead moving the college to longer term, renewable non-tenure track contracts. This might have been attractive, and there are legitimate arguments that perhaps this is the direction that academic work should move into in the future. But for me, I did not really trust that this was a viable option, or one that would be especially long lasting.

All of my intellectual work ceased; all of my academic life came to a close. I did not know what to do now that I did not have tenure, and I still wondered what it meant that "there was nothing I could do" to get it. Should I work on more writing? Should I get a lawyer and challenge the process or the decision? That was, I knew, a very long shot. There was no issue of racial or gender discrimination in the process. I suppose that there were procedural questions that might be raised but the courts have not been particularly responsive to those demands by aggrieved professors. It was now fall, the job-hunting season started but I had not fully prepared for a job search. And, since I had family commitments, I could not see how I could possibly move anywhere in the country to take another position should I even be competitive enough to get an interview and an offer.

Do job committees want to know about tenure decisions? And, in my case, I had not been "denied" but I had not been granted tenure either. How was this to be explained in searching for a job? Who can I talk to about this? Friends helped but I did not personally know anyone who had been denied tenure or had the same issues as I did with the process. After all, like Hardy's character in "The Dead Man Walking," the denied are the "shape that stands here / A pulseless mould, /A pale past picture, screening / Ashes gone cold." We are not much wanted around. We continue to teach and occupy an office at the institution but we should be unseen. We are just ghosts. Unwanted ghosts. Senior members of the college and department offer measured sympathy but not much guidance. Younger members see the taint that clings to me and to my case. Positive tenure decisions are announced. Negative decisions, with good and logical reason, are not. People still want to know but are fearful of asking. Why was he denied, they whisper? How might I avoid that fate? No one wanted the details of my case rehashed. Those details concerned only me. Certainly, being seen or engaged in deep conversation with me could not possibly be a good thing at the college. I might have a lawsuit in mind. Best not to engage. Stay clear. Stay away.

> *But when I practised eyeing*
>     *The goal of men,*
> *It iced me, and I perished*
>     *A little then.*
>
> *When passed my friend, my kinsfolk,*
>     *Through the Last Door,*
> *And left me standing bleakly,*
>     *I died yet more...*

—excerpt from Thomas Hardy "The Dead Man Walking"

In truth, I could not really expect my colleagues old or young to help. None of them had been denied tenure (they were still at the institution obviously), and my college had not had a failed tenure case for a while. And, in any case, I was not really in a position to ask that they put me in touch with anyone. We are left on our own in this process. This is probably the biggest struggle of those going into the tenure process at any institution and, even more so, for those that are among the denied.

### Advice From The Denied

There are two areas that I would highlight from my own experience that I think apply more broadly to rethinking the tenure process at institutions (if not even the tenure system more broadly writ). The first is mentorship. I had no mentorship through the process, and there is certainly no mentorship when it goes wrong. A robust mentorship process would, I think, help all young professors going through the tenure process understand more of the workings of their chosen profession and their specific institution. Second, there needs to be a broader sense of career paths within and beyond the tenure line. No matter what is done to modify, reform, or rethink the tenure process at any institution and the tenure system across the university landscape, it is most assuredly disappearing. Some proclaim a deep fear at the potential loss of tenure—ironically, it seems to me, since the system is not actually particularly old (the AAUP dates to 1915; the modern tenure system to about 1940 or perhaps even more post-World War II). Others celebrate tenure's collapse and destruction, although those revelers at tenure's funeral do not offer much hope of protection for academic work outside the mainstream or protection for those who speak out against harmful institutional practices, policies, and problems. But both groups know that the tenure system as we have known it for about the last 60 or so years is most certainly going away. We need to train our graduate students to enter and understand that world and that reality.

Mentoring is an area that is currently a mishmash of confusing and contradictory policies across institutions of higher education. Many places make some nodding attempt to describe a mentoring process for junior faculty but they have little to no institutional heft or large-scale institutional presence. In many cases, the only mentoring programs happen informally from within departments or they happen not at all. In other cases, formal mentoring does take place but only within the department—that is a start but also ignores the enormous potential for conflict of interest from within a departmental program. Institutions that lack a substantial number of women faculty or faculty of color, for example, might not serve the interests and needs of junior faculty by simply pairing them with the gray beards (often white men) of the existing departmental structure. Although departmental advice and counsel are good and necessary, they do not make for much of a thorough and complete mentoring program.

Although there have been some developments in mentoring over the last decade or so, there is still a woeful lack of information, training, or assistance in this area. It seems that it will all simply "just happen." I have even noted programs at a number of universities that put the onus for mentoring on the junior faculty member. These programs encourage the junior member to pursue a mentoring relationship—and even offer a small measure of funding to seek and develop these contacts—but, again, this is simply institutional avoidance. The junior faculty member—if we are to believe the three-legged version of tenure that is so often celebrated—must *publish*, must provide *service* to the department and the university, must *teach* their courses, and must mentor their own advisees and students (and in PhD and/or MA granting institutions, graduate students). Now, at institutions with these programs, another job is to find and develop a mentor relationship through the tenure process? What exactly is the university/college doing to develop careers other than judging them at the end of seven years?

There needs to be much more systematization of the process of mentoring faculty. If the tenure system is worth saving and protecting—and I think that it is despite my own failures within it—then larger institutions need to be involved in the advocacy and encouragement of these changes. The university and the college are the first place to start (and not only the department). But extra-institutional groups also bear some burden. The AAUP cannot simply suggest that they advocate for an effective tenure *system* but do not say much about the institutional tenure *process*—leaving that up to the individual college/university in the hopes that the faculty at those places serve as creator and protector of the tenure and promotion process. But, of course, the faculties are not really the largest stakeholders in the tenure process in the current university despite what they might think about their relationship to it. The faculties do not structure admissions decisions or allocation of students (or student dollars) across the institution; the faculties do not review or necessarily have significant input on the allocation of university financial resources across the institution as a whole; the faculties do not manage institutional decisions on large capital expenditures. These are administrative decisions. And tenure is, in the end, a decision finalized in the administration not in a faculty promotion and tenure committee. In my tenure case, I was effectively denied at the administrative level after every faculty committee—the departmental, the college, and the university promotion and tenure committees—made its decision in my favor. When you add questions of equity—racial, sexual orientation, gender—the institutional tenure process (not just the nationwide protection of the tenure system) becomes even more fraught. These were not present in my particular case but are certainly—and much more often—the arenas of conflict, bias, and denial. And they also need to be parts of the mentoring process as well.

The AAUP is not the only institution empowered to deal with the systemic issues within the tenure process and tenure system in higher education. Discipline based professional associations have the power to advocate for the professionals that they represent. In some cases, this is improving—the American Historical Association, for example, did a few reports on tenure and promotion processes in the last ten years—but this could certainly be more robust and would be further encouraged by a mentoring program that provides education, access, and information to those on the tenure track. The associations might make issues of tenure and promotion regular items on any conference agenda. They too can mentor. They too can speak to the issues of equity. And they can do this every year that they meet. They meet for scholarship every year; they meet for new work in fields and subfields. If anything is a consistent issue across the university landscape it is tenure, promotion, employment, and career paths.

In addition to the need for institutions to better mentor junior faculty once hired—and to mentor them across the institution and not just in the department—graduate departments need to do a better job of training their students to be more than tenure track faculty in each and every discipline. If they do not know how to do this, or do not know where the resources are to pursue this preparation, then they need to find it, develop it, and make it part of their educational charge. To individual professors, I would recommend that they constantly think about job skills beyond the tenure line – they tie you to a broad community beyond academe and they help prepare you should something go wrong. If tenure denial comes, or even if your life and career desires simply shift over the course of years of education and work, you will be much better off if you are prepared to enter into other kinds of work.

This process was rather haphazard in my case, and mostly the product of luck and not forethought or planning. I worked in various professional capacities on AP grading and development, on editing a professional society's newsletter, and in engaging programs to improve my teaching. I imagined these as professional service within my discipline and institution, and to a certain extent they were just that. As it turns out, they also provided me the cushion of skills that I now use in my current position in an independent secondary school. In fact, these skills helped me on the market after tenure denial. It is hard enough to attract interest in a job in higher education when you do not have the whiff of tenure failure, are years older than other candidates, and have personal obligations that might complicate the location of any search. I knew that after my tenure debacle a future in higher education was probably out of the question. But I quickly realized that my graduate degrees, years of teaching and writing, and service within my discipline were not necessarily the aspects of my work that attracted interviews and interest outside the academy.

Instead, it was the skills I developed alongside those other aspects of my time in higher education that provided the most benefit in my job search. And I still think that I was mostly lucky. If I had come out of my graduate education, however, better prepared for the reality of life on the tenure track I would have needed less luck. My department did not discuss work options in my field outside of tenure track employment. There was talk in the 1990s, when I was in graduate school, of putting in your time as a visiting professor or adjuncting. But the Holy Grail was tenure track employment, which these short term stays, we were led to believe, only made more likely. They helped you pay your dues, as it were, and trained you more as a teacher, scholar, and professional. We now know that these did not translate into a greater likelihood of employment, and I have heard more than one colleague note that the collection of visiting positions hindered their career.

We also did not speak about teaching in another level of education. We rarely talked about employment outside education. In my years of graduate training I remember one talk from a museum professional about their work. Moreover, the department celebrated the tenure track hires of its graduates. It did not promote with the same vigor employment elsewhere. As anyone who has been in a graduate school program knows, however, there are always fellow students in your department who finish their dissertations and do not have permanent or perhaps even any employment. Sometimes, in a few years, you hear they landed a job and the department celebrates. Other times, they seem to disappear, just like the ghosts of the denied after a failed tenure review.

These students do not seem to be invited back to discuss what they have done with their careers. They might be bitter but I think that the bitterness is more directed at the fact that they were not prepared or trained for this. If the only training is to become a tenure track faculty member, and you are not a tenure track or tenured faculty member, it is clear the department does not believe you are its poster child to speak to its current students. If departments, chairs, and graduate advisors do believe that tenure track employment is their purpose and function, then departments across the university know they are serving, celebrating, and educating about 30% of their graduate students. Because that is roughly the number who might end up in a tenured or tenure track position. In some fields, the numbers are even worse.

Broad training and mentorship will make for better professors and for better professionals in disciplines across the university. It certainly makes for a better environment within a department. Years of graduate training, teaching, and writing should not be deemed a failure because one particular type of work was not achieved. Perhaps, it should not even be pursued. When I see large numbers of PhD's granted in my field, I wonder what those departments granting those PhD's are doing with all those graduates; where goes what William James called over a century ago the "PhD Octopus"? Where are these students working? How many of them have ended up in the permanent state of per course, part-time adjuncting? How many might have gone into other aspects of their disciplines if their departments had made that an equal measure of their time?

As with the issue of mentoring, there is some movement to think more broadly about employment and assistance. Career offices are starting to offer resume services that go beyond university employment. When I was a student, the career office was oriented entirely around employment for graduating seniors seeking their first job or internship. The career office offered graduate students a dossier service for collecting a teaching portfolio, recommendations, and a curriculum vitae. Great if you were seeking a professorship. Fairly useless in other kinds of job searches or other arenas of work. Graduate students with Master's degrees or PhDs are not looking for the same work as undergraduates.

Recently, there have been a number of articles in the *Chronicle of Higher Education, Education Week*, and elsewhere, reporting on the push to improve graduate student career development. This also needs to be institutional and not departmental. For years, jobs were simply discussed within departments, the information on who went where was never tracked or collected. Institutions should have to do this as a matter of course and fair reporting to its current and its future students. Graduate students and their professors should demand this be an institutional effort to track the careers of those who receive degrees. Professional associations should also make it part of their charge as well. Career centers should be created with personnel dedicated to working with graduate students in all aspects of their careers. If the universities will not do this, it should be crowd sourced—which the *Chronicle of Higher Education* briefly did in 2013—and published until the universities pursue the data themselves.

## LIFE OFF OF THE TENURE LINE

I did recover from my tenure denial eventually. I am not the "corpse-thing" anymore of Hardy's lament. I do not suffer from the "live not now" conclusion of his poem. I have found a new career, a satisfaction, and a purpose. I am writing again—this essay is part of that attempt. My old unfinished book, tattered remains of which are in files on my computer, in my Google drive, in Dropbox, has returned to the front of my mind. I might finish it. I might write something else. In that sense, I suppose this essay has the happy ending of the tenure denial essays that appear now and again in print. That is a good thing, I think. There is nothing wrong with having success pointed out and celebrated. Although I attribute much of this to things outside of my control and training.

But the larger conclusion that we can draw is that this is a broken system that does very little to develop, train, and sustain careers. There is no reason why the process that I experienced needs to be in place. Moreover, I would still be considered rather lucky. I had a teaching position for multiple years at one institution. This is not the characteristic path coming out of graduate education any longer. At least two-thirds of graduate students employed in higher education will be part-time or partially contracted; they will likely experience a lengthy process of chronic underemployment. The tenure track job cannot be the only career focus of graduate students or graduate departments any longer. If that is what academic departments think that they train, then they will be leaving behind far too many people.

I think this is an important moment in educational training and employment in the academy. I see little discussion in the defenses of keeping tenure of how the process should be made better, made less opaque, or part of graduate student training through the PhD process. There are nods to fairness and consistency, but I do not generally see this translated into a broader graduate student career education and formal university mentorship programs. But the defenses of tenure as a system and a process should include these and other systemic changes. Those who desire tenure's destruction or celebrate its demise should also push institutions to better prepare their students for the reality of academic employment today (not its reality in the past), and broaden the way we conceive of professional success within our disciplines. Either position requires the universities and colleges to change, and, I think, to change soon.

## She Who Is Looking Her Age

### J.W. Young

My mother left when I was an infant, and my father was serving a 101-year sentence in a California State Penitentiary. I was raised by my grandmother, whose favorite hobby was to take me to May Company, have me try on clothes, and veto each outfit by saying, "You look like shit in that." Her other hobbies included criticizing me about my love of language, stories, and reading. I liked these things, she said, because of my thick thighs and round ass, because I was offish and so unlike the fine-boned girls at my school. She often pinched my fat legs to show me what she meant. If I protested, she pinched me harder, leaving bruises.

But the two criticisms I heard the most—that really burned because they were true—were that I didn't belong among the "good" (read: normal) class of kids, and that I had to keep my mouth shut and fake like I did so I'd get the same advantages. I was trash, my grandmother told me. And if the other kids never realized it, and I never said otherwise, I'd get by, get along, go farther. So I did as she said, I kept my mouth shut and believed. Because she was in a position to know. She wasn't trash. She'd had a mother and father, and had lived in fine homes, and worn furs, and been given furniture from John Wayne. I was only good enough to clean John Wayne's table, not sit at it.

Keeping quiet made life easier in our home. Backtalk was met with backhand violence and a two-day tirade meant to remind me that I was trash and if I didn't keep my big mouth shut I'd really get into trouble. People would suddenly not want anything to do with me once they knew my secrets.

I never offered up anything personal about myself to classmates and potential friends, nothing that would later on allow them to betray me. And the quieter I was, the more obvious it became that it was right—girls betrayed each other over petty grievances, like failing to sit at the "right" table during lunch, or "stealing" a third-grade boyfriend. Those girls came from two-parent homes, never raised a finger to help with housework, had never mown a lawn or painted a wall. These were more secrets I kept about myself. I nodded and smiled and avoided eye contact. And I was accepted in their academic circles, the only ones that mattered. Education, Grandma said, was the only way out for a girl like me. I took advanced courses, made straight A's, burned those perfect-family girls to the ground. I was at the top of my class. If they'd found out I was trash, they would've ostracized me.

I remained quiet far into my young adulthood—longer than I should have, really. Into college and graduate school, and even after I'd been a tenure-track English professor for a few years. Long after it should've been clear to me that I was smart and did belong among the academic elite. Long after I should've realized that Grandma was wrong about people. Academics weren't classists. I didn't need to hide who I was, my lineage, for them. Pedigree was on its way out. What mattered was intelligence.

\* \* \*

When I encounter some women my age—generation Xers or those on the far cusp—who don't pump their own gas, have never refinished furniture or poured concrete, I find them perplexing. They empty litter boxes, then congratulate themselves by drinking entire bottles of wine. They take criticism personally. They don't handle stress well. My entire childhood was an experiment in stress-survival. So, I never had girlfriends. But when I began my position as an Assistant English Professor at Middle Georgia College, and I met Crystal O'Leary, she made it clear we were going to be friends whether I wanted it or not. "When I saw your teaching demo," she said, "I told the VP, 'We need her. She's fantastic.'" At the time, I didn't recognize this comment as a you-owe-me-your-job jab, but she repeated this story many times over the years that it soon became obvious she was pinching me under the table, congratulating herself, not me.

"All these men around here will think we're at each other's throats if we're not friends," she said. "They'll assume we're jealous of each other and can't work together. Everyday they'll be waiting for a catfight. I'd rather not play that game."

Crystal had been a debutant and was a member of the Junior League. She often quipped about how she'd stayed in college on "Daddy's money" which resulted in her "prolonged adolescence." She majored in theater, then got two more degrees, and became a professor because she didn't know what else to do with herself. She laughed about the fact that her parents had given her the down-payment for her house. She couldn't fathom buying one on her own, the way my husband and I had. Each time I spoke with her at work, I had to remind myself to keep my mouth shut. The only difference between her and the lunch-room girls of my youth were years.

I quickly became well-liked by my students and colleagues. I published, attended conferences, revived the literary journal, and began a reading series that eventually brought a Pulitzer Prize winner to our tiny campus. When I wasn't teaching, I was writing. When Crystal wasn't teaching, she was drinking. When I wasn't writing, I was reading Southern authors like Faulkner and O'Connor. Crystal bragged that she'd never read a single Faulkner novel. She preferred stories written by members of her "gaming" group that met each Thursday night to discuss how their vampire avatars would make it through a quest.

I'd never planned on marrying or having children. But I'd stumbled upon a loving man, and then had a beautiful daughter. Crystal, though, thought of marriage and motherhood as gold medals in need of winning. She was pushing forty and hadn't landed a mate.

She said things like, "I wish I had your enthusiasm." She seemed genuine.

As did everyone else in our Division. Because I'd faked belonging to a group for all of my twenty-eight years, I never thought I'd find real belonging. Especially since the higher I climbed in academia, the more elite my colleagues became. Most of them came from academic or upper-class families. Even the "struggling" artists had aunts or grandfathers with street names or church festivals named for them. Though I felt smart and had even been promoted to Associate Professor, I didn't feel like I belonged.

But I got tired of keeping quiet. I started churning out narratives about my young adult life and growing up. Several of them were published. Three essays were anthologized, and a few colleagues taught them in class. One asked me to deliver a brown-bag lecture on "The Art of the Essay" that was attended by faculty, administration, and students. Then a few of us, including Crystal, formed a writing group. She always showed up with helpful feedback and constructive criticism, but seemed hard-pressed to produce anything herself.

One of her earliest betrayals came after our group had been meeting for a year. I was approached by a friend of hers, a colleague uninvolved with our group with whom she'd shared my writing, who proceeded to tell me how I should've rebelled as a teenager, quit working so hard. He couldn't believe I was actually from the "working class." He thought, because I was white, married, and an academic, that I was from the same privileged class as he and Crystal. He spoke as if voyeurism was some sort of legitimate critical analysis. He ended his one-sided conversation by telling me that Grandma had been wrong about the world, perhaps even abusive.

I'd lived through the events in my essays and was attempting to turn them into the beautiful songs they hadn't been when they happened. I considered all of my writing malformed until I got acceptance letters, and only shared pieces with the group. Most of the other writers knew that discussing work outside of our meetings was not acceptable. Apparently, Crystal didn't. And instead of mentioning it to her, I fell back on my habit of keeping quiet in the presence of someone who wasn't trash.

The group dissolved a year later, but Crystal insisted I keep her up to date on my publications. She'd email the faculty about them, and even though publishing wasn't part of the Promotion and Tenure guidelines, it would make me "look good" she said. Still, I couldn't shake the feeling that she was watching me with a little too much awe.

\* \* \*

When our Division Chair left MGC, Crystal decided she'd apply for the job. She told me, "I had a long talk with Daddy. He thinks this is the right thing for me to do. He said there's not much else for me here." It was the same sort of thing I'd grown up hearing—Mommy and Daddy thought little Becky was talented. They threw money in her general direction and she got what she wanted.

After she'd been in the position for a few months, I explained to her that, like family, friends weren't meant to be bosses or business partners. I expected her to agree. But she told me I was being ridiculous. We could still be friends, she'd said. She'd insisted. She'd cried.

Shortly after her promotion, the College began its Quality Enhancement Plan (QEP). As one of her first new duties, Crystal put forward my name to chair a sub-committee. "If you don't take it, you'll be committing career suicide," she said. "It's your decision, but I strongly recommend you take the position. It'll assure you get tenure." I took her advice. Work on the committee—to research, plan, coordinate, create, implement, and assess learning communities across the curriculum—began to take up much of my time. There were only four members and we juggled coordinating classes, recruiting faculty, creating campus-wide programs, collecting data, and writing reports. At every QEP meeting, the VP made it clear that the work we were completing was crucial for the College's accreditation. Crystal began to say I was being "groomed for administration" in the cynical, pinching way Grandma used to tell me to keep quiet. My anxiety spiked. I spent long hours and weekends working on the QEP. My writing fell away.

Because I couldn't commit time to composing long essays, I began a blog and started a Facebook page. Of course, most everyone I worked with used Facebook. We were all "Friends" online. And at nearly every faculty meeting, Crystal reminded us that while there was no official social media policy, any association with the College on our pages could be misconstrued. "But I guess if you don't have the College listed in your information, it's not a big deal," she said. I knew most of my colleagues hadn't taken any precautions, but I made sure I didn't mention the College anywhere. Nor did I even use my real name on my page—I used my pseudonym. My only identifying marker was my profile picture.

But then I read an Emily Post article that suggested not being Facebook friends with your boss or most other people in the workplace. The argument was that Facebook suggested equality, something that didn't exist between a supervisor and her employees. I contemplated it for many weeks, trying to keep Grandma's voice from taking over the narrative. But eventually I began to "unfriend" colleagues. I called Crystal one weekend and told her I was going to unfriend her, too. I explained that it wasn't personal. "That doesn't make any sense," she said, near tears. "I can be your friend and your boss."

"I don't think so," I told her. I tried to convince her that I was right, but the more I pressed, the more I felt like I was saying too much. I kept her as a Facebook friend.

\* \* \*

Shortly after her marriage, Crystal began trying to conceive. She came by my office to describe her struggle, conversations that made me squirm not only because I found them inappropriate for the workplace, but because my daughter's pictures were all over my office. Then one day she told me she was a month pregnant. She was so excited, she'd already told her parents and in-laws. But the next month, she had a miscarriage. She didn't want me to tell anyone at work, and it was easy for me to keep quiet. Several months later, when I invited her to my husband's birthday party, she declined by saying that she couldn't celebrate because that was the week her baby would've been born. Six months later, when I asked her if she'd like to babysit my daughter, she told me, "I just can't be around kids anymore." I began to read books and articles about how to help someone through that grief. I said the things the books and articles told me to say, but she told me I wasn't helping.

Soon, her visits to my office tapered off. I'd pass her in the halls and she'd hardly look at me. My colleagues commented on how the job seemed to crush her. "Crystal's really looking her age," one of them said. They complained about her poor performance, and I commiserated because twice she'd mistaken email from a colleague as email from me. She was unable to communicate College policies, and was irritable and grumpy. I wanted to excuse her because of the miscarriage. She'd been so devastated; she'd referred to her womb as a "graveyard." But I couldn't betray her. And because she didn't talk to me anymore, I didn't really know if the miscarriage was actually causing her unhappiness. The Chair position seemed more like the culprit. She openly complained about it, the hours, the other Division Chairs she was forced to work with, that the VP and President were simply expecting too much from her, and that she couldn't do anything without the Division secretary—a woman who'd been on the job for twenty years.

That year, the College faculty were bullied into revising the Promotion and Tenure guidelines. At a campus-wide faculty meeting where we met to discuss and vote on the document—drafted by the President and his counsel—many of my colleagues openly took issue with the addition of the word "collegiality" used in a subcategory of one of the four major review components. Unlike "Effective Teaching" and "Commitment to College," they didn't understand how "collegiality" would be assessed. The President stood at a podium and said, "Do you really want to work with someone who doesn't fit in?" He was met with silence.

"It's a popularity contest," Crystal said through clenched teeth. She disliked the President and had been vocal about her fears that if she didn't do what he wanted, she'd lose her job.

The new Promotion & Tenure guidelines were approved, and when I complained about the decision on Facebook, Crystal unfriended me within twenty-four hours. When I called her and asked for an explanation, she coldly told me that she didn't think my criticism was appropriate. It brought me to tears because I'd remained friends with her against my better judgment. I felt like she'd been waiting for an excuse to unfriend me, and because of my big mouth, I'd given it to her.

My relationship with Crystal continued to deteriorate over the next year. She became openly hostile toward me, but always made sure we were alone when she was—in the building's elevator, in the copy room, in the restroom. Each time I published an essay or organized a campus event, she sarcastically called me a "rock star." When I expressed interest in the Governor's Teaching Fellowship, she told me I wouldn't be able to attend unless I completely rearranged my teaching schedule to include two night classes. When I challenged her, pointing out that our Faculty Handbook encouraged enrichment, she told me, "I've already made accommodations for your lifestyle choice."

"What 'lifestyle choice'?" I asked.

"Having a child," she said.

I was stunned silent. I'd never considered my daughter a "choice." Having a child was, for me, a miracle because I'd been told I'd never conceive. Finally, I said, "I'm not sure I understand what you mean."

"I won't approve your application," she said, ending whatever chance I had at the prestigious appointment.

I sent her an email about an adjunct's tirade toward a staff member, during one of my QEP events. He was belligerent, I told her, and students witnessed it. She accused me of trying to do her job.

In front of other faculty members, she'd say, "You're such a superwoman—mom, teacher, writer—I just don't know how you do it all," mockery oozing from her mouth. I'd bite the insides of my cheeks, the way I had as a girl, and smile through the pain.

*　*　*

That year was also the first and last chance I had at gaining tenure, so I worked on my application packet for a month. I emailed Crystal several times for clarification about the new policies, and each time she assured me I was doing everything correctly. Several other faculty members in my Division used my packet as a template for their own. I submitted long before the deadline, then watched my calendar. I knew the Division committee would meet early in the fall, and then Chair recommendation letters couldn't miss the November deadline. The College-wide committee would make their decision in January, write their summary, and submit that to the VP who would then submit her recommendation for the President's approval.

Just before our December winter break, Crystal cornered me in the copy room and said, "Another Chair and I are drafting an Intellectual Property policy for the college. You should know that the College may be entitled to any money you make on a publication, especially if they can show they gave you compensation like a course release or paying for a conference. I know you're working on a book, so I wanted to give you a heads-up."

I was shocked stiff and stood in the room for a moment trying to understand what she'd just said. I'd told her only a few days before that I was going to attempt compiling some of my essays into a memoir about growing up as an inmate's child under Grandma's roof. She'd told me she'd like to read it when I was finished. But now she seemed to be accusing me of something. Finally, I managed to say, "Um, is that even legal? How would they prove 'compensation'?"

"You write in the summer."

"And?"

"The College pays your health benefits in the summer, so if they wanted to they could say they're entitled to profits. Like I said, I'm helping to draft it and I'll do what I can. In the meantime, just be careful."

That afternoon I sent an email to friends at other colleges. I asked them what policies were in place, and each one responded that publishing was just part of the job. One of them encouraged me to "get far away from there if those are the sort of people in charge."

I was furious. What she'd told me didn't seem right. But more than that, it bothered me how she'd delivered the message—with no witnesses. I thought about it for weeks, growing increasingly frustrated and angry. Eventually, I blogged about how "blind sighted" I'd been. And I did a bad, bad thing. I opened my big mouth a little too much. Rather than using her name, I characterized her as "she who is looking her age."

In late January, Crystal called me into her office to discuss that blog post. She accused me of fabricating the entire Intellectual Property conversation and of being uncollegial and "sowing discord" within my Division. "I bet you never thought I'd see what you wrote," she said. Each time I tried to defend myself, she cut me off, saying, "Be quiet, this isn't time for you to talk. Just listen."

I'd posted information about a policy the College was drafting, she said. That was "sowing discord" and creating a "hostile work environment."

"But you just said I made it up," I managed to say. "Which is it? Did you tell me about it, or did I make it up?"

"You're twisting my words," she said. Her hands were shaking and she rubbed them together. "Be quiet."

"No. You're calling me a liar and I didn't lie."

"Be quiet. This is not a time for you to talk. You'll get your chance when I'm done."

So I sat and listened to her diatribe. She went on and on about my inability to communicate effectively. She brought up my Facebook complaints about the new P&T guidelines.

"Wait a minute," I said. "You never told me any of this when it was happening."

"I unfriended you. You've got a pattern of this sort of poor communication."

"I don't have a 'pattern.' You're making one. Why are you talking about Facebook?"

"Be quiet," she said.

"Quit talking to me like I'm a kid. I really don't know what you're upset about. I'm sorry I called you a name, but I'm not the only one doing it. People talk about you behind your back all of the time. It's part of the job—"

"Thanks for letting me know."

"You're welcome," I said, just as sarcastically. By then, I knew I was out of line. But I'd had enough. She sat behind her large desk, with a title she hadn't earned, intermittently rising as if she was going to lurch at me, then sitting back down and staring at a scrawled piece of paper—one that looked more like her husband's handwriting than her own—and would raise her voice when calling me a liar. She looked like every girl I'd had to kowtow to all of my life.

Eventually, she allowed me to speak. I said, "If you're so concerned about what I write on my blog, maybe you should read some of the other stuff there. Or do you only read the posts that have something to do with the lies you tell me?"

"This meeting is over," she said.

The next day, I went to Human Resources and looked in my file for reprimands or negative reviews. There were none. I searched my Division file for the same. There were none. There was no pattern. Crystal simply wanted "she who is looking her age" off of the internet. As did her husband, who sent me a threatening email from his work account accusing me of blurring the line between work and friendship. My description of his wife, he said, "will not stand."

I revised the post and removed "she who is looking her age."

*  *  *

Three months later, Crystal came into my office, sat down opposite me, and with a slight smile on her face announced that my tenure was denied and I had to resign. I wouldn't be able to get another job in academia if I didn't, she said. There was no appeals process, no further review, she said. When I asked for an explanation, she told me I wasn't entitled to one. I spoke to a lawyer friend that evening who told me that, under the Georgia Open Records Act, the College had to produce my finished Tenure packet within seventy-two hours of my request for it. I received the paperwork a day after my request. Though I'd had overwhelming support from the Division and campus-wide committees, Crystal had blackballed me because of "she who is looking her age." Her letter of non-support outlined in three paragraphs what she'd said to me at our meeting and offered no evidence for her claim. Additionally, it was dated a full two weeks after the November deadline. Though the faculty had been told deadlines would be upheld, her letter was allowed to be submitted fourteen days late.

Was I culpable? Absolutely. I opened my big mouth. I characterized Crystal as she was being spoken about in the halls of our building. And that still goads me; I wish I'd come up with a better insult, especially since it cost me my job. I might've thought of something with flare, something that really sang. Instead, I used the banal language of others, a description that even her husband recognized.

Did I deserve to lose tenure? A lawyer said no. My colleagues said no.

But enough of my upbringing had shown me that the answer was yes. I knew that opening my mouth, exposing myself, was stupid. One tongue-wag out of line with Grandma and I went to bed without dinner, woke without breakfast, and tried with everything in me not to inhale my school lunch lest the "good" girls find out I was trash. I learned to nod, and listen to her tirades, and when she went into one of her manic episodes, try to stay out of earshot of her wicked tongue. I learned to smile in front of everyone else, to work hard, to keep my head down.

I suppose, I was tired of Grandma being right.

A year after I left the College, it was swallowed up in a consolidation and now no longer exists. The President was terminated, the VP was demoted, and Crystal was stripped of her position. The new institution drafted different Promotion and Tenure guidelines which eradicated the collegiality clause. All of these things should make me feel vindicated. But they don't. Mostly because no one really knew what happened to me since I kept silent about it. The same way I kept silent in my childhood. I've kept silent for so long about growing up, some of my own family members don't believe me. I was clean, quiet, dutiful. I never got into trouble with teachers and excelled in school. I looked like a child with an overprotective parent. Not like a kid with an ulcer, a sleeping disorder, and severe depression.

The year before my daughter was born, Grandma died suddenly of a massive heart attack. The paramedics who tried to revive her said that her heart had exploded. A few days before, I'd spoken to her on the telephone and she'd cried because she'd forgotten to send me a birthday present. I assured her that I didn't care, that I'd outgrown birthday celebrations. I said this not because it was true--but because my heart couldn't withstand her sobs. The anguish she felt, the humiliation, it came out in a flood of tears, and later it caused her own heart to shatter. I'd like to say it was then that I understood how much I loved Grandma, and how much I pitied the mother she'd been to me. She'd cast into me all of her own fears, tried to make me the perfect child. But I couldn't remain little forever, despite her best efforts. No, I didn't understand the love I'd had for her until the day I left MGC, nearly six years after she'd died. When I turned in my keys and said my goodbyes to my colleagues, Crystal hid in her office, her door open so I'd know she was inside and wasn't going to come out and face what she'd done. And I was suddenly struck by the memory of Grandma's crying, her insistence that she was sorry, as if she'd been apologizing for much more. It's her cracking voice that I associate with my last day.

I would've continued to keep silent about what Crystal did had I not learned that she now tells people that I attacked her for no reason. She'd always been a good friend, she says, and I am a bad person. Perhaps I am bad. Perhaps I am trash. But I can't keep silent anymore. Especially now that I have a new position, at a smaller school, where my colleagues are professional and friendly. I teach, I write. I've since had twins. I'm publishing again and have finished my first book. And I couldn't have made this better move, to an environment that embraces me and my hardships, without She Who is Looking Her Age. She may have been the best thing that ever happened to my career.

I haven't seen Crystal in five years and my anger toward her has crumbled away. My departure set her fragile world at ease. I'm no longer the constant reminder of the world at large, the things she didn't have to endure as a child and young woman, the milestones she failed to achieve. But life is not a straight race, with medals won at steady intervals of time and place. Life cannot be contained, segmented, awarded, the way Crystal thought. Life is, sometimes, even running backward, turning in the prize and forgiving the judges for their mistakes, even when they'd convinced you that you're unworthy. Life is knowing that you're not who they think you are.

# The Mean Girls' Club at Red County Community College

*Madeline Grey*

> *Failure is becoming someone*
> *who needs others to fail.*
> —Alain be Botton

The gallery at Red County Community College was hosting an art exhibit featuring scenes of the flora and fauna of the Susquehanna River Valley. My photography would be making its debut appearance. I was hoping that the sales of my photos would raise money for a student scholarship in the English Department, where I'd worked for four years.

A day before the exhibit opened, the gallery director rejected one of my photographs, and I was supposed to pick it up from his office. When I'd approached him a few months earlier about raising money for a student scholarship by exhibiting my photography on campus, he'd asked me for some local nature scenes. But now he'd rejected an image entitled "Hope Is the Thing with Feathers" which captured a swan on a nearby lake, a lake so close you could see it from some of the windows on campus.

"What happened with this one? It's local. Branford Lake. That's right around the corner from here," I asked him.

"Swans aren't native to the U.S.," the gallery director informed me. "They're an invasive species that came here in the 19$^{th}$ century from England."

"Yes, but they live here now, don't they? And they have for two whole centuries. Seems to me they're a part of the local environment."

He stopped what he was doing on his computer and looked at me clutching the framed photo.

"Listen," I pleaded, "you said you wanted to help me raise money for a student scholarship. If I'm going to sell any of my photos, it's going to be this one. I'll even take down one of my smaller ones."

"Okay, okay," he acquiesced. "You can put it in place of one of your others."

By the time I'd hung it where a smaller photo of the Susquehanna shoreline had been, somewhere else on campus three members of the English Department had met privately and decided to nix the student scholarship for which I was fundraising and for which I'd received a favorable, nearly unanimous vote at the department meeting the previous day. Before I sold my first photo from the exhibit, the series of events that led to my tenure denial would have unfolded.

\* \* \*

There were no photos on the walls of President Dickerson's office. Instead, they were decorated with awards from the Chamber of Commerce and the Downtown Business Association.

"My real job as college president here," he pontificated, "is to separate rich people from their money. The more wealth people have, the more unhappy most of them are. And that's the key to fundraising. You have to convince someone that giving away his money will make him happy. And usually it does. It unburdens him from his guilt."

I was taking notes on what President Dickerson was saying, but I wasn't entirely sure why he had requested to meet with me. One day I had come to campus with copies of a journal that had published an essay I'd written about my father's service in Vietnam, and as I descended the stairs on my way to teach, I passed President Dickerson. I stopped him and pulled a copy of the journal out of my bag. He'd taken it with a promise to read it, but I never thought he would. A couple of weeks afterwards, his secretary wrote me, saying that the President wanted to meet with "the famous author." I thought they were joking. But it wasn't a joke. No one in the English Department of the community college ever published anything. So with one essay, I was some kind of celebrity. Or, perhaps more accurately, I was an anomaly for which they could not account.

So I sat there listening to him talk about fundraising, telling me that he thought I had a real future at the college.

"What are your plans?" he asked me. "Have you thought about getting involved in college administration?"

"Well, it's been hard to think past my tenure application coming up in a few months," I confessed.

"Oh, you'll be fine," he assured me. "You'll get tenure. If you need anything, just ask me. We want to hold on to someone of your talent."

And then he told me a story about Vietnam that should have taught me everything I needed to know about him and about my lack of a future at the college.

"I was in Vietnam, you know, like your dad. But I was a pilot, not infantry. Do you have any idea why we went there, why the U.S. invaded?"

"I assume it had something to do with money."

"That's right. Drug routes," he said. "And I will tell you what. It was not a dignified war. Nixon said when we withdrew that we would have 'peace with honor.' There was no honor to what we did. They made us leave behind our men. Our commanding officers gave us orders to pull out while we could see our friends on the ground. Those soldiers did everything we asked of them, and we left them behind."

To say he was getting choked up would be an overstatement, but there was an intensity to his gaze. He'd ditched his fake smile. It was the first genuine moment of feeling I'd witnessed from him. The rest of it had all been administrative hot air, political posturing. This was why he'd called me into his office. Because I'd written about my dad's service in Vietnam and how it had changed him.

"Well, thanks for coming in to speak with me." He reached out to shake my hand as I stood up. "Do think about getting involved in some aspect of fundraising on campus. And try to keep your distance from most of the people in the English Department. They're a little nuts."

\* \* \*

One of the people he surely meant for me to keep my distance from was the President of the Faculty Union, Michelle, who was one of the most senior colleagues in the English Department. Michelle had almost no family and only a few friends. What few friends she did have put up with her, it seemed, because she bought them things, often expensive things. She took me to lunch a few times and seemed to want to "mother bear" me, which was the nickname given to her by a junior faculty member who was denied tenure two years before I was.

"Don't worry," Michelle said over pasta primavera at her favorite Italian place, as I stressed over my tenure application. "Jia, that junior faculty member who was denied tenure, always missed her office hours because she had a kid and lived over an hour away."

I rolled my eyes at this news. It didn't make me feel any better that she was discriminated against for being a single mother.

"She wasn't the greatest teacher," Michelle continued. "Her teaching evaluations reflected that. You have nothing to worry about—your evaluations are great."

At our lunches, Michelle would tell me about the awful bullying she had survived in the department, mostly from her female colleagues. The ones who had gone after her were almost all retired now, but we agreed that the culture remained. In fact, it often remained in the victims of it, who turned around and harassed the next batch of junior faculty, like the cycle of abuse in a family.

"They probably did discriminate against Jia on numerous fronts," Michelle admitted, "for being non-white, for being a single mom. They've learned to get away with it. Partly because we haven't been able to be as effective as we'd like as a Union."

I'd not received much of the bullying yet at that point, only heard about it, from Jia, mainly, who had made the egregious professional error in a right-leaning region of trying to stand up for diversity on campus. She'd chaired an unpopular committee on diversity and had inadvertently insulted President Dickerson's wife, who was the head of some fancy ladies' garden party organization who put Christmas decorations up every year in the mansion building where our offices were located. It was such an overblown affair—with a different themed Christmas display in every room: the bows, the live poinsettias, the golden trumpets and ivory angels—that Jia had apparently said with disgust that it "looked like the Victorian era threw up in here" and wondered aloud about why the garden party ladies don't also decorate for Kwanza or Chinese New Year.

Michelle said she tried to stand up for Jia, but there was only so much that could be done. Despite some reservations, the Department recommended her for tenure. Then the college committee had also voted in favor. But President Dickerson vetoed it. And he had the final say. No ungrateful Chinese-American would be messing up his white Victorian Christmas.

Prior to Jia, another young woman was chased out before she even went up for tenure. The final straw in her case was that she had posted to social media about the bullying she'd received from senior female colleagues, who had been trying to impose their way of teaching on her as the "only right way" to teach. I first heard about this criticism from the mouth of one of the accused senior colleagues, Karen, a loud-mouthed woman who swore like a trucker and who thought that a form letter rejection from *The New Yorker* was enough to qualify her to teach the only poetry writing class at the college even though she'd never published anything.

I'd only been teaching there a few weeks when she confided in me.

"Some junior faculty just don't appreciate our mentorship. I hope you won't be one of those," Karen said ominously. Karen was best friends with Beth, the newly appointed Chair of the Department. They had worked their way up from adjuncts and thought that made them the only "real" teachers, even though they'd both been trained decades ago and didn't keep up with current developments in pedagogy.

I honestly tried not to be "one of those" junior faculty. Which meant I followed every asinine piece of advice they gave me. For example, Karen observed one of my writing classes and didn't like that I was teaching a separate unit dedicated to revision strategies before paper revisions were due at the end of the semester. "You're ghettoizing it," she accused me. "It's better if you do it like I do and weave it in throughout." And then Beth, my Chair, decided that she didn't like that I accepted papers through the Blackboard course management system offered to us through the college. She told me that I had to stop collecting papers electronically, that I could only accept them in hard-copy. So that's what I did.

Beth admitted that she was ethically opposed to collecting student papers via Blackboard or Turnitin in order to help detect plagiarism, because, she said, "It assumes that students are going to plagiarize."

"So does having a plagiarism policy on our syllabus," I told her, which the college required us to have.

\* \* \*

Despite the President's fundraising efforts, and despite how fancy the mansion was that housed our department, our classrooms were pitifully outdated. The computer monitor stand was broken in the one classroom I used. Someone had propped it up on a roll of paper towels so we could see the screen. Most days, either the computer or the projector wasn't working. Usually a few days every semester, the water in the building turned dark brown and smelled bad. All the administrative offices had deliveries of bottled spring water brought in.

But spring semester in the year before I applied for tenure, the computer completely stopped working in my classroom. The students groaned every time I tried to turn it on—a running joke between us. How long would it take for IT to fix it? We started taking bets. But despite my work order requests to IT, the computer remained broken. I requested a classroom change through Beth to be able to switch to one that had a working computer, as there were some available down the hall at that time. Beth approved my classroom transfer, and for the second half of the semester, we mostly had a working computer in the classroom, although if I was showing anything with sound, I had to bring the pair of portable speakers we shared between the faculty in our department because the computers in our classrooms had none.

I thought I'd handled the computer issue marvelously, following the chain of command, solving the issue. But at the end of my yearly report, Beth added that I was "overly reliant on technology" because I had needed to use the computer in my classroom. I went to her office with a copy of the report.

Beth was stuffed into the seat at her desk, layers of dark clothing spilling its wooden arms. Sitting down, she wasn't as comical as when she lumbered around the spaces of the historic building in which the Department was housed. Her large facial features and belly, towering over her tiny legs and feet made her resemble the character of Witch Hazel from the Bugs Bunny cartoon.

"Beth, the fact that I taught over half the semester in a classroom without a working computer, while still achieving the learning goals of the class, would actually prove the opposite of what you've written here."

She looked at me like a cow chewing cud.

"Don't you get it?" I went on. "I taught the class perfectly fine. You have no evidence that proves otherwise. And I did it without access to a computer for six weeks of the semester."

"You need to trust your Chair more," she snapped.

The sad truth was that Beth, the Chair of the English department, my boss, would probably not have been able to pass my freshman composition course, given her inability to perform simple logic. It was a wonder to me that anyone had given her a Master's degree. But that had been decades ago. She wouldn't have made it through any respectable graduate program now.

On my way back to my office, I passed a window that looked out onto a sliver of Branford Lake. I wanted to fly far away from this place, but with teaching five and six courses a semester, I had only managed to get out a handful of job applications that year.

*  *  *

Bullying by the members of the English Department came in many forms. My lunches with Michelle turned abruptly awkward; she started insisting that I go on a date with a student who was taking her class. He was an older guy, about my age, who shared many of the hobbies that interested me. But he was a student at the college where I taught. I understood that Michelle was trying to look out for me, trying to do a nice thing by helping me find a boyfriend. But it felt very strange to be talking about dating a student at the college, even though he wasn't a student in my class and never would be, as he was done with all of his English classes. Not to mention, this request was coming from the President of the Faculty Union! And she was losing her patience with me. Finally, for fear that it would be detrimental to my career if I didn't, I agreed to go on a hike with the guy on a weeknight after school. We spent most of the time talking about strategies for his application to the radiology program. Afterwards, we exchanged a few text messages, and then we lost touch.

A few days after the hike, Beth called me into her office and gave me a lecture about not dating students.

I stopped talking to Michelle.

It was impossible to avoid her completely in the cramped space our department occupied on the third floor of the mansion. Sometime in the next semester, as I was making my way hurriedly to the copy machine, I passed her as she was in conversation with someone else. We mutually ignored each other.

When I returned to my desk hugging the still-warm copies, Michelle stomped into the office I shared with four other people.

"How dare you pass right in front of me without acknowledging me!"

"I'm sorry," I said. "You didn't acknowledge me either."

"I won't be treated this way. I'm your senior colleague, the President of the Faculty Union."

I looked at her without saying anything—my best "you've got to be kidding me with this" face.

She leaned in closer. "If you pass me again without saying 'Good morning,' I will file a complaint against you for a hostile work environment."

"You mean like the one you're creating for me right now?"

She turned on her heels and left.

I was called into Beth's office later that day and given a lecture about how I had to pay proper respect to my senior colleagues. With all the ego drama going on in our department, I was starting to understand why no one ever published anything or had time to present at conferences.

And that's eventually what sank me. The publishing. Attending conferences. The kinds of professional activities I'd always been encouraged to do, which were now an affront to my colleagues, an indictment of them.

They tried to make it about my teaching, but they couldn't get me on anything. I was observed at least three times a year. All stellar observation reports. Even from Beth.

Another senior colleague, Anna—a short, white-haired, stern looking woman who fancied herself in charge of everything, who was good friends with Karen and Beth, asked me more than once, "you do know, don't you, that this is a teaching institution?" whenever she'd heard that I published something, even a poem. Especially a poem, because Anna considered herself a serious poet, even though her work had only ever appeared in little booklets she'd printed up herself.

Like any hypocrite, Anna didn't really believe what she was telling me. Her email signature line proved that. It read like an Act of Congress. And it didn't list the classes she taught—even though (didn't she know?) we were supposedly at a teaching institution. The list that followed her name on emails went on and on with all of the committees (and sub committees) and statewide faculty governing bodies she was serving on. If she got onto a new one, her email signature would immediately be updated—I saw one go up as early as 48 hours after she'd been nominated to chair a special task force. (It was simply a task force meant to ascertain how faculty felt about a proposal to build a new dorm on campus.) Her bio on the college website would also be updated weekly, it seemed, with the latest version of the list of committees she was involved in, information most of us had never even included on our website bios, let alone updated. I hadn't added anything in the four years I'd been there, and I'd published two handfuls of essays and poems, plus a peer-review article in an edited anthology, and presented papers at national conferences yearly. I didn't even know whom to contact at the school to change my online bio.

And it was Anna's jealousy that would be my final undoing—Anna, who had been denied tenure herself at the community college in her hometown in upstate New York.

I used to believe her story about what happened there. But now, I'm not sure what I believe. Her version of the story is that she was bullied by the Provost who wanted her to give another chance to a student athlete who had failed the final paper and therefore failed her freshman composition course. According to her, she "stood by her standards" and was denied tenure for it. What I missed about this story the first couple of times she told it is how anti-student she sounded, how she cared more about her "standards" than she did about learning experiences for students or about being a team player. I think it must have been after being denied tenure that she became the very thing she supposedly hated—the administrator who bullies young faculty into doing what she wants. It must have been then that her ego became so fragile that no amount of good work could make her feel like she was enough, that the only way she could feel like she was enough was to tear other people down, especially good people.

* * *

It wasn't just the Mean Girls' Club of Anna, Karen, and Beth who made my life difficult at Red County Community College. The men were equally bad. The former Department Chair who hired me was most likely sleeping with one of the junior faculty in his campus office. He had been ousted as Chair for it in the middle of his term.

And then there was Ruiz, a tenured developmental English teacher whose Master's degree was in Music. Ruiz was also a representative in the Faculty Union. He was in charge of sexual harassment disputes, which basically meant that he knew exactly how to sexually harass women faculty and get away with it. Ruiz was also the head of the social committee, a position that gave him the excuse to throw his own little VIP parties, selectively inviting only the faculty who were in his good graces.

Ruiz was always on the make. Once at a happy hour during fall semester, after I'd taken a glassblowing class the weekend before, I was telling a small group of my colleagues about the process of shaping and handling the pumpkin paperweight I'd created. Ruiz chimed in.

"I've never wanted so much to be a pumpkin," he said, "so that Lynn could blow me."

At another happy hour, I'd shown up a little frazzled from a hard day of teaching and my hair was falling out of the braid I'd put it in that morning. After I arrived at the bar for happy hour and placed my drink order, I excused myself to go to the ladies room to fix my hair. Ruiz stepped in and said, "No need for you to leave. I can fix your hair for you." Then he approached me from behind, rubbed his hands on my shoulders, took off the elastic, and undid the braid by running his fingers through my hair. He played with my hair for another few moments before guffawing and stepping away, "Yeah, I don't know how to braid hair. I just said that because I wanted to touch you."

Ruiz was the Mean Girls' Club pick as representative to serve on the hiring committee. After he was voted in (unanimously—even I voted for him since the vote was public and no one who wanted to keep his or her job could cross the Mean Girls!), I returned to my office and mentioned to another colleague that I was worried about how Ruiz would handle himself on the hiring committee if an attractive young woman were to be brought in for an interview. Someone reported my comment to Beth, who told Ruiz. Ruiz confronted me.

"I could file a harassment claim against you for what you said," he told me.

And according to Beth, he was considering it, and I was going to be in big trouble because I had expressed concern about the professionalism of a colleague who had sexually harassed me multiple times. Good to know the Union was looking out for faculty.

* * *

Despite all of the bullying and sexual harassment, the malfunctioning technology, and the time the college had (without warning) sprayed my office sprayed with an incredibly toxic pesticide that left me unable to breathe the air in there for a week and which got onto my student papers and books, and which possibly contributed to heart abnormalities afterwards that required follow-up care with a cardiologist, I continued to excel at my job. In fact, while teaching five and six classes each semester at Red County Community College, I still managed to uncover and deal with numerous cases of plagiarism. I became rather good at sniffing them out, even though it was time-consuming sleuthing. Funny font changes and strange characters inserted into the document were red flags, but it might take two hours of research to locate the original material in order to build a case. I didn't normally spend that much time per paper trying to catch plagiarism, but it was my job in freshmen composition to teach students how to properly document their sources. I'd had teachers from other departments look me up, after they saw I was the instructor on a student's transcript for the freshmen composition course he took, and ask me why Johnny hadn't learned to cite properly. So I felt a lot of pressure to do my job of teaching students not to plagiarize. Usually, if I caught a freshman composition students doing it, I just had him or her redo the paper after using it as a lesson in what plagiarism is and how to avoid it.

One student I caught plagiarizing, though, was in an upper-level course and had a full scholarship at Duquesne University for the next year. When I showed her what she had done, she feigned ignorance: "I don't know how that happened!" As this was her first offense, I asked her to resubmit a different, non-plagiarized paper. Essentially, I gave her the second chance that Anna had refused to give her student-athlete, the situation that had supposedly cost her tenure. It did little good. My best student then handed in a paper she'd copied word-for-word from the Internet. I was then required to launch a full-scale investigation, re-examining the other papers she'd handed in earlier in the semester. One of them had also been cobbled together from Internet sources that were used without citation. This was the third plagiarized paper she'd handed in to me in the course. Three strikes.

I went to Beth and explained. She gave me the green light to contact Student Judicial Affairs. On my way out of Beth's office, I ran into Anna and told her, without naming the student, that one of my best students, a student who had a full scholarship to Duquesne, had plagiarized three papers in my class. Anna hurried in the direction of her office with a quizzical look on her face.

Student Judicial Affairs found the student guilty of plagiarism and expelled her from the college. She didn't even bother to show up to the hearings they scheduled. She would never go to Duquesne.

At the college-wide assembly in August, during the opening general announcements from the floor, Anna stood up and addressed everyone.

"I just wanted to thank the office of Student Judicial Affairs publically. I discovered a case of plagiarism last semester in one of my classes. The student in question had a full-ride to Duquesne University. "

My eyes narrowed.

"So I want to thank Student Judicial Affairs for having my back and for doing the right thing in expelling the student after such an egregious case of academic dishonesty. By enacting this punishment, they sent the right message to students."

I asked the new hire sitting next to me if she knew what Anna was talking about.

"Yeah, apparently, she caught a student plagiarizing in her Ethics Class—like every paper. The student lost her full scholarship to Duquesne because of it. It's so ironic, you know, because it was Ethics class."

It was very ironic, indeed. Very ironic that Anna, the biggest traitor of all, was teaching an Ethics class.

As we filed out after the meeting was over, Anna sidled up to me. She was giddy.

"Just so you know for the future," she smiled triumphantly, "the administration likes to hear that kind of praise."

Any hope I'd had of being appreciated for my efforts at Red County Community College was gone. I was dealing with pathological egoists who wanted to claim all of my hard work as their own.

And if they couldn't claim it as their own, they would deny me the opportunity to do it.

A few months after the assembly meeting where Anna took sole credit for the plagiarism case I'd discovered, the student scholarship I'd proposed was introduced and then voted on as an action item at a department meeting. Anna made some mild remarks against it. Not only did she consider herself the unofficial department photographer, even though her photos had never been part of an exhibit, she was also normally in charge of fundraising for student scholarships in the department, even if someone else was head of that committee now. In the past, Anna had made large posters on which she'd hand-drawn a thermometer and colored it in red with each hash marked donation amount until the goal was reached and the picture of the thermometer fully colored in. I was proposing that we use the sale of my photography on campus and an online funding campaign, not hand-colored posters. The vote passed, with only two abstentions. But I had forgotten how resistant the Mean Girls' Club was to technology.

Later that night, Anna and Karen went to their buddy Beth and the three of them decided to show me that I wouldn't be allowed to do anything that they couldn't take credit for. The next day we all got a memo saying that there had been some objections to the scholarship, from Anna and others, after the department vote and that Beth was going to veto it.

Veto it? I thought. That's not how Robert's Rules of Order works. That's not how departmental business is conducted. Why would we even bother voting at meetings if the Chair could just decide procedure behind the back of the rest of the department?

In the meanwhile, I'd gotten an email from Anna asking me to call her about the scholarship. I emailed her back and asked why she wasn't more supportive of my proposal for a scholarship. She wrote back saying that she refused to talk about it over email. I replied that I was in an area that did not have great cell service and that I wasn't interested in having this fight with her. I asked her for one good reason why she opposed my raising money for our students. She forwarded my email to the Dean with a charge that I was harassing her, that she felt threatened by the tone of my email. Anna was the former President of the Faculty Union. She knew what she could get away with. To make matters worse for me, our current Dean was a graduate of Red County Community College—a blonde, Kewpie-doll of an administrator, who couldn't seem to make any of her own decisions, and she had been Anna's student.

Michelle, the current President of the Faculty Union, the one who'd tried to play matchmaker, called me as soon as she heard. "Can we bury the hatchet? I'm really sorry for what I did, and you're going to need my help."

I was brought before the Dean and the head of Human Resources for a disciplinary hearing. Michelle came with me. The Dean tried to convince us that the tone of my email was unprofessional. I kept asking her to point to some word choice or style that was unprofessional.

"Did I use all caps? Did I bold anything? Did I say anywhere that I was going to hurt Anna if she didn't support my proposal? No, I did not."

"But it's just your general tone of voice that's unprofessional," the Dean whined.

"How can you tell tone of voice from an email?" I asked again. "In this email, I specifically say that I don't want to fight with her. You'd think that would suggest the opposite of a threatening tone. I'm telling her that I'm not going to engage her with hostility."

"If you have to qualify your tone, then it means the tone is wrong."

"Or I'm just being truthful and telling her how to read this email. Tone is very difficult to read in emails."

The head of Human Resources jumped in.

"You think you're better than everyone here, don't you?"

"No, I . . ."

"You think that because you have a PhD that that makes you better than all of us."

"I never said that."

"Well, I think that you have to be a very bad teacher." She thumbed through my file. "How can someone who is rich enough to have a PhD possibly understand our working class students?"

I was shaking. My parents were first-generation college students. My grandfather had died of black lung from working in the mines. My grandmother had dropped out of high school and worked as a factory seamstress—she made a nickel for every zipper she put into a piece of clothing. And I was the first person in my family to earn a PhD

"I challenge you," I spoke slowly, taking frequent breaths to calm myself, "to find one criticism of my teaching. You won't find it. And moreover, I find your logic appalling. I'm $60,000 in debt for my PhD."

The head of Human Resources was also a graduate of Red County Community College. I'd never been treated so unprofessionally by college administrators in my life.

As Michelle and I exited the meeting, walking toward our cars, I began to cry.

"Come here," she said, and gave me a hug. "They did to you the thing I had threatened to do."

She was right. She'd felt like I hadn't kissed her ass enough, just like Anna felt that she was beyond my reproach, that merely calling her into question was subordination, even if there was no logical argument that she could possibly make against my raising money for a student scholarship. None of this was about logic. It was about ego. About a bunch of small-minded female colleagues who'd been empowered by bullies and who had then become them.

Karen looked at me with genuine concern and pity. "Didn't you say your photos are up now as part of the exhibit?"

"Yes, it opened last week."

"Come on, show me your work."

We entered the gallery, and Michelle caught her breath as soon as she saw "Hope Is the Thing with Feathers."

"Is that yours?"

"Yes, it's a photo I took of a swan taking flight. It was just around the corner here at Branford Lake."

"I have to have it. How much?"

"Well, it's listed at $200, but for you. . ."

"Nonsense. I'll go tell the director right now that I'm buying it."

\* \* \*

A few months later, Anna—who had gone behind the back of the department and, with the help of Karen and Beth, sabotaged a democratic vote—won some award for governance, and the department voted to approve me for tenure. The College Committee did the same a couple of months later. The President, who was very close to the Dean and the head of HR, vetoed my tenure application two weeks before Christmas, as his wife was puking Victorian Christmas all over the mansion. My buddy, President Dickerson, the one who had asked me to get involved with fundraising in the first place, had sold me out. The only reason ever given to me was that "my interests, like publishing and attending conferences, seemed were more suitable to a 4-year institution." The Dean provided me with a stellar letter of recommendation, which she then withdrew after she found out I'd contacted a lawyer. I was unable to sue because the terms of my contract were such that they could let me go at any time prior to tenure, even for just disliking the way I breathed air.

In a final act of incompetence, the Human Resources office mistakenly sent me the wrong termination paperwork with someone else's name, address, and social security number on it.

I imagine President Dickerson there on the floor of his mansion looking out through the window that would give him a glimpse of Branford Lake. But then the window morphs into the windshield of a jet. Through it, he can see a platoon of soldiers coming out the trees, taking heavy fire. They'd fought so hard to get to that clearing—good people, who'd been through hell. And they were counting on him, counting on his assistance. His radio crackles with orders from his superior officer, telling him to return to base. He turns the wheel and the wing dips as he leaves his men behind in Vietnam.

But in the case of my tenure denial, he had no commanding officers to blame for giving orders. I'm skeptical now about the story of his service, just like I'm skeptical about Anna's tenure-denial story after I saw that she'd become the very thing she purportedly hated. That President Dickerson had orders to leave his men in Vietnam was beside the point—it was an excuse. He was the kind of person who betrays the folks who have done everything they'd been asked. Beth, Anna. . . they all were that same kind of person, eager to remove anyone who could challenge their incompetence.

These are the kind of dysfunctional people who are promoted to positions of power now in academia, at least in non-research institutions. Forget being a good teacher, forget being a good writer. The more mediocre you are, the better off you will be, because you won't threaten any of the senior professors or administrators. If they're jealous of your good work, you become a target. At this historical moment in higher education, at regional institutions like Red County Community College, incompetence and pettiness are protected and valued more than intelligence and success. The anti-intellectual backlash we're seeing in popular culture is understandable when these kinds of ego-politics represent the face of higher education to many working-class people.

# The Thing With Feathers:
## My Five Years at a SmallChurch College

*Nancy McCabe*

"You can't do that! We don't do things that way here!"

It was my first day at my first tenure track job, and all of the senior members of my new department were shouting at the other new hire, a Shakespeare specialist I'll call Caddy. Had Caddy just announced a plan to conduct closed-door conferences with her most attractive students, using her newfound status as a professor to seduce them? Had she revealed her intention to teach naked while twirling loaded firearms?

No, Caddy had simply mentioned that her students would be writing a lot of papers.

As the hubbub died down, each senior colleague patiently explained. Only in-class writing was allowed, and only in conjunction with "objective" tests, and only in an idiosyncratic four-paragraph, conclusion-free form based on a long out-of-print textbook. This is the way the department had always done it.

And these expectations clearly applied to me, too, leaving me stunned and puzzled. This new department had, upon hiring me, told me how excited they were to bring someone in with recent graduate training and twelve years of experience teaching creative writing and composition. But now it appeared that teaching writing was actually prohibited. I'd been so excited and hopeful about this new job, for which I'd moved, alone, halfway across the country. And now I wondered what I'd gotten myself into.

\* \* \*

In 1996, when I'd finished my PhD, the job market was terrible—fifty openings in my field that year, more than a thousand related degrees. Among the many application letters I wrote was to a small college in the South which I will call Pulpit University, or PU. I received a confirmation in the return mail. By the way, the letter said, all PU employees must be members of a Christian church. I tossed the letter into the pile of materials for jobs I'd decided not to pursue, and forgot about it—until the day that Quentin, Pulpit University's search chair, called.

"We'd like to bring you to campus for an interview," he said.

I hesitated. I knew I'd better be honest quickly, before I could think too much about the dismal job market.

"I'm not an active member of a Christian church," I blurted out. "I joined my childhood church when I was twelve, but that probably doesn't count."

There was a long pause. "Well," said Quentin in a soft Southern drawl that sounded only mildly startled. "We'd like to bring you anyway." The undercurrent of amusement in his voice decided me.

I flew from the Midwest to the South on a 19 degree February day, shedding layers across the country: the heavy coat stayed in Omaha, I peeled off the long underwear in Detroit, and by Atlanta, I'd stuffed my sweater into my carryon. Here it was 70 degrees, and daffodils were blooming. For years I'd lain awake at night, worrying about my future. Here, it was spring and I felt new hope.

During my two days of interviewing, English department members hastened to assure me that the church membership requirement was nominal, and to many of them, objectionable. It didn't limit anyone's academic freedom; it didn't stand in the way of free thought and broad inquiry. The department co-chair, Jason, told me that he had not himself been in a church since sometime in the 60s. Quentin the search chair admitted that during the last few years—since receiving tenure, I found out later—he'd been "exploring his Jewish roots." In other words, he attended a synagogue and observed Jewish holidays, in addition to speaking at conferences about Jewish literature. But he, like me, had joined a Christian church as a child.

When I arrived for PU's new faculty orientation, I wasn't asked to sign anything or make a statement of faith. So I was a baffled when the dean mentioned that in defining who was a Christian, the college followed military policy.

"Don't ask, don't tell?" I asked.

The dean winced. One of my new colleagues kicked me. The dean cleared his throat and stumbled out an explanation. He was referring to some policy that classified Methodists, Episcopalians, and Baptists as Christians, but excluded Mormons, Jehovah's Witnesses, and Unitarians. Recently the list had expanded to include Catholics.

That was only the beginning of my culture shock. A native Midwesterner, I was frequently lectured on the importance of good manners in the South, graciousness being equated with subservience in minorities and women. During a discussion of pedagogy, one male colleague insisted that it was reasonable to expect female faculty to take more time with students and be more nurturing while male faculty attended to more important matters. After all, he pointed out, women were the ones who had babies. Men routinely addressed each other by titles—"Dr. Carothers" and "Dr. McAslin"— and women colleagues by our first names. Party invitations arrived for faculty and our wives. Janitors refused to clean the offices of female faculty members.

One day at the dining hall, a colleague lectured me about why the inferiority of women was a legitimate theological perspective. And whenever anyone mentioned the need for diversity on our 98 percent white campus or 75 percent male faculty, others cautioned, "We must not worship at the altar of diversity."

"I don't think we've entered the foyer of diversity yet," I said once. Nobody even cracked a smile in response.

"Actually," a colleague earnestly told me, "the trinity is quite diverse, since it embodies a father, a son, and a holy spirit."

From the first day when I discovered that I was not really allowed to teach writing, I frequently found myself in the midst of generational, cultural, pedagogical, theological, and/or theoretical clashes. When I'd first signed my contract, my new department had told me that they hoped I would help them reshape their freshman program. It wasn't immediately clear that my colleagues meant someday, maybe in about ten years, after many of them had retired, but I was fine with that. I had no wish to change them. I did, however, expect autonomy in my own classroom, something I'd always taken for granted, even as a 22-year-old graduate student.

But sure enough, students were only allowed to write in the approved departmental form, and we were to grade according to a rigid point system that emphasized superficially polished products over processes that might lead to deepened critical thinking and more sophisticated work. I was told to avoid the process methods that had dominated composition studies for decades. I was expected to abandon the portfolio assessment that had revolutionized my own teaching.

I'd been assigned a class called Literary Criticism, a required one for English majors, mostly because no one else wanted it. I was instructed to emphasize New Criticism and downplay current approaches, in particular, feminist ones—the ones I, with PhD specialties in women's studies and women's literature, was most qualified to teach. Many department members believed that classroom discussions were a fruitless pooling of ignorance. To them, effective teaching consisted of lecturing to upper-level students on terminology with which they were intimately familiar and on how "experts," primarily New Critical ones, had interpreted the literature.

Collisions of old and new, traditional and progressive may be inevitable when freshly-minted PhD's from research universities join the aging faculties of small institutions. Conflicts are bound to arise between people whose training occurred thirty years apart. At the same time, even many seasoned traditionalists would have been exasperated by the essays my PU students had been taught to produce, mechanical, formulaic exercises that reflected no depth of thought. I thought that English majors should be pushing their ideas in more sophisticated and original directions. We did writing exercises toward that end, and I also incorporated peer review sessions as well as small group proofreading work.

"She's not doing things the PU way," some students complained to my supervisors because I was responding to content instead of just grammar, emphasizing process and not just products, and leading discussions more often than I lectured. Along with units on psychoanalysis and Marxism and deconstruction, I included a unit on feminist theory, presenting it as the pervasive and influential school that it was, which, some students concluded, meant that I "hated men." Better students rose up to defend me.

As if even the natural world begrudged change, the leaves and grass on my route to school remained startlingly green for weeks. Every day I drove under those eerily green trees canopied over the highway. I passed green kudzu twining around branches and furring telephone poles, stalled in time. I took refuge twice a week in my poetry-writing class, burgeoning with enthusiasm, discoveries, breakthroughs: no one could say I wasn't doing a good job with it, at least.

My small department liked to compare ourselves to a "family," and it was true that we were a somewhat dysfunctional group stuck together in close quarters day after day. Years later, writing about my department and choosing pseudonyms for my colleagues, I drew from Faulkner's *The Sound and the Fury*'s Compson family. Caroline, our female chair, could be stern, severe, even merciless, a predator of obscure grammar errors and minuscule policy violations, but she was maternal and obsessively fair and had, against many obstacles, established a women's studies program on campus. Jason, our male chair, wanted to be seen as at the forefront of progress but was so set in his ways, he blocked every change he championed. He was always wringing his hands at opinions, teaching methods, critical approaches, or life priorities that differed from his. His reputation for brilliance was based on the dramatic, polished style by which he delivered the same lectures he'd been delivering for thirty years and his chief writing strategy consisted of impersonating someone British.

Other members of our dysfunctional family included Auntie Maury, who wore black and cultivated a mild, agreeable dementia in order to avoid extra duties and campus politics. Big brother Quentin was typically clad in jeans and tended to be off elsewhere, avoiding conflict and exploring his Jewish roots. Big brother Benjy was a slight hearing impaired guy with a large collection of vintage cars he drove around town on Sundays and an even larger collection of bow ties. There were also a couple of non-tenure track faculty members who went about their business quietly.

When we expressed concerns, senior colleagues told Caddy and me how lucky we were. At one time, it had been common for faculty to rage into each others' offices, demanding to know things like, "How dare you pass a student who doesn't know the difference between present gerunds functioning as adjectives and present and past participles serving as substantives?" Former department chairs had regularly blown up, stormed, scolded, slammed doors, banged down phones, and screamed at colleagues who ended sentences with prepositions. We agreed dubiously that yes, we were lucky.

\* \* \*

"What is that?" Caroline shrieked.

We were in Big Brother Benjy's immaculate kitchen, preparing for the department's annual Christmas party. Once again, everyone's horrified attention was focused on Caddy, who had placed her offering on a silver serving dish: a big orange nut-coated cheeseball.

"That's not British," Caroline said, mock-severe, her tone the kind of joking humor one uses to cover others' shocking errors in judgment and gruesome faux pas. Caddy had been assigned to bring cheese, me dessert. No one had told us that the meal was supposed to be traditionally British.

"Aren't we supposed to have Stilton?" Jason said.

Caddy had gone pale and still. "No one told me," she said.

It took her a while to realize that she wasn't going to be fired on the spot. So far, most of the negative attention had been focused on Caddy's mistakes rather than mine, though there was an undercurrent of displeasure that I had brought cookies from a family recipe; the seniors wolfed them down at the expense of a big bowl of trifle. But no one said anything to me, though the next year Caddy and I would each be given more specific assignments. Mine was to pick up jugs of iced tea from a local barbecue joint. "I had no idea they drank so much sweet tea in Dickens-era Great Britain," I said, but no one cracked a smile.

At the end of that first party, after all of the students had departed, Caddy and I tackled the stacks of dishes in Benjy's kitchen, me washing, her drying. At one point, we burst into the *Laverne and Shirley* theme song:

Give us any chance we'll take it, read us any rule we'll break it. . .

Caroline and Jason passed by, bearing dirty dishes, smiling nervously.

The spring was something of a relief, with a brief reprieve from micromanagement since I was teaching no required courses for English majors. In department meetings, I tried to ignore Jason's jittery shifting, furious hair-pulling, and pained high pitched emissions when confronted with any opinion I expressed. Any negative student comment had him pacing around glaring at me and muttering dire pronouncements to colleagues about my incompetence; he dismissed positive comments with a low growl: "Student evaluations don't mean anything." He scolded students for "dumbing down" when they enrolled in my classes—especially if they dropped one of his to do so.

In my end-of-the-year review, the dean sighed during a discussion of English department dynamics and said, "People retire." That was the standard line across campus in response to frustrations: "People retire." I understood by now that this meant to be patient, bide your time, things would improve someday. "You are the future of PU," the dean said to me, and I felt hopeful again.

Until early the next fall, when I made an offhand comment in a meeting about my students' peer review process and chaos ensued.

"Why would you do that?" Caddy and Quentin exclaimed; even they sounded scandalized.

"How will students learn to proofread if we don't work with them on strategies?" I asked.

"That's a violation of the honor code!" Benjy yelled.

"How will you prepare students for my upper-level classes if you don't enforce the Departmental Grading Guide's penalties for grammatical errors?" Jason roared.

"But the Grading Guide goes against all of my training," I said. "It focuses on correctness, not on development of ideas."

"How dare you question the way we've been doing things for thirty years?" Jason was turning red.

"I understand that you want to teach writing as a process, but that sounds like cheating," Caddy said.

"Allowing students to read and help correct each other's work is plagiarism," Caroline said. "How do we know they won't steal each other's ideas to improve their own work?"

"But that's how scholars work," I protested. "They challenge each other to complicate their ideas and they build on each other's—"

"This undermines the very foundation of our department, this college, and our profession," Jason thundered.

I sat blinking, shocked and horrified, rendered speechless and close to tears.

The next day, Jason and Caroline whisked me off to Sizzlin Sirloin for lunch. There, Jason growled, "Who do you think you are? Your job is to teach the terminology and in-class writing skills necessary to prepare students for the rigor of my classes. Period." He looked on the verge of a stroke.

Caroline gently intervened. Surely I could compromise, combining Jason's approach with mine: I could assign out-of-class essays and give in-class essay tests. I could both lecture and lead discussions.

I tried to reconcile the idea of helping students develop ideas through multiple drafts while also insisting they write fully-formed, sophisticated, well-structured, perfectly-punctuated essays in ten minutes. According to departmental policy, out-of-class and in-class writing must be evaluated on the same standards. Senior colleagues maintained that the policy raised the level of in-class writing. It seemed to me to instead lower the quality of out-of-class writing. And while I already incorporated mini-lectures into my class format, if I switched my primary mode to lecture, setting myself up as the ultimate authority on how students should read literature, wouldn't I cancel out the benefits of leading discussions that assisted students in working out their own interpretations?

But Caroline had made a decision. "That's it, then. Jason, she'll add some in-class writing and some more lecture to what she's already doing, OK?"

I tracked down Quentin, who rarely lectured or gave in-class essays himself. "If you want to keep your job, you're going to have to abandon any integrity you thought you had and do what they say," he told me.

My literature students took in cheerful stride the abrupt addition of graded in-class writing halfway through the semester, an essay on Emily Dickinson's "Hope is the Thing with Feathers."

The next day, Jason announced that he was going to observe my class. After a small initial panic, I decided to use the session to follow up on the essays, which I called a "test" for Jason's benefit. I confirmed that most of the students had correctly identified the form as common meter, iambic tetrameter alternating with trimeter—the hymn stanza.

Jason was smiling. He liked terminology.

The students had mostly interpreted the poem as a happy, pretty one about the redeeming power of the human capacity for sustaining hope despite all else. I moved through the poem line by line, pulling in their essay responses as I summarized the ways that their variety of answers connected to, reflected off of, resonated with, and enriched each other. I was teetering along a fine line: aiming to continue a discussion by quoting from student responses while simultaneously convincing Jason that I was lecturing.

I pointed out observations that students had made about the relationships between form and content, about how at first glance the poem's three four-line stanzas appeared simple, regular, traditional, unthreatening—yet how the slant rhyme in the first one signals that something is amiss, that we should pay close attention to currents running underneath the poem. We talked about the image of hope as a caged bird, singing a tune without the words. What did that imply? That hope was a pretty, fluttering creature, brave and resolute, never failing—but does the speaker unquestioningly admire that bird? How does she feel about the storm that she describes as "sore" for daring to "abash the little bird" that "keeps so many warm"? Did my students detect any irony there, any tongue-in-cheek commentary that presents the storm as a mean bully daring to try to destroy an emotion we'd prefer to cling to? What does that say about how hope can interrupt our willingness to face reality? Is hope only a blessing, or does it carry negative aspects?

Jason had been nodding slowly, approvingly, at first, but as the room began to crackle with energy, his nods became manically enthusiastic. He raised his hand and I called on him.

"Remember that when Pandora let loose all the evils of the world, what she found at the bottom was hope," he said.

"Does that mean that hope was one of the evils?" I asked. "And if so, why?"

Students jumped in with comments, questions, and elaborations, piggybacking off each other, quoting from the poem, offering insights about the ways hope can lead people astray, can lead us to hang on when we ought to give up and change directions, how it can keep us from accepting things as they are.

Gradually, the strands of our discussion came together. While Dickinson celebrates the human capacity for hope, she's also a bit skeptical of it, suggesting that if it can survive without even a crumb of encouragement. In that case, does it sometimes amount to self-delusion? Can maintaining hope despite constant defeat ultimately be more destructive than giving up?

Beaming, Jason made his exit and the class heaved a collective sigh of relief. We had all kicked ass and we knew it. But I also felt like I'd just run thirty miles in the last thirty minutes: awed, triumphant, but gasping for oxygen and on the verge of heart failure.

Jason told Caroline and Quentin how impressed he was. My students wrote glowing evaluations of the course. And for me, the effectiveness of prewriting exercises to jump start a discussion had been reinforced. Now, I thought naively, my future was assured; my department would leave me alone to get on with my work. My hope once again began to soar. I was going to make things work.

But it didn't take long for my stress level to rise again. My chairs kept throwing extra tasks and assignments my way that no one else wanted and that Caddy was excused from so she could finish her dissertation. I organized a reading series, hosted visiting writers, sponsored a creative writing club, worked with the student literary magazine, ordered most of the contemporary literature for the library, designed and taught a research methods course, served on the education committee, attended two-day state meetings to establish standards for education entrance exams, and prepared to undertake my department's education accreditation portfolio, all while teaching every creative writing course along with literary criticism and freshman classes covering ancient Greek works, medieval epics, Shakespeare plays, representative Romantic and Realistic works, and contemporary literature.

And as I fought to keep up with the work, it sometimes seemed that any stray, seemingly innocuous incident could throw me into disgrace, like when I gave a B on a paper to one of Jason's pet students. All of a sudden, junior colleagues skittered away from me like scared mice while senior colleagues failed to greet me in the halls and Jason paced by my office door, glowering, arms folded.

Going to work felt treacherous. On the road to campus, mica in the pavement winked like fragments of knife blades. The ground, scattered with acorns, rolled under my feet. Doors swelled and shrank in the humidity, never fitting their frames the same way twice. I developed constant hives to accompany an ever-present stomachache. I read the next day's assignments in oatmeal baths and took half doses of Benadryl so that I could stay awake to read more.

One day, Big Brother Benjy invited me to lunch. He cooked a thick stew in his spotless kitchen and beamed at me as we ate. He confessed to me that at first he'd thought that my tactlessness was a character failing, but he'd come to understand that it was a result of the geographic region that had formed me. Midwesterners were just tactless people. I was startled, seeing myself as a relatively direct but kind person. Benjy beamed and said that he hoped he could cook lunch for me again—as a Southerner, he loved to be hospitable.

"Tactless?" I asked Caroline. What could I possibly have said?

She didn't know for sure. Once I'd admitted I didn't like a book it turned out that Benjy loved, and he looked crushed. And once I'd told him that after renting my apartment sight unseen, I'd been afraid I would arrive and say, "Oh no! What have I done?" Benjy then told everyone that I hated the school, state, and region and was going around moaning, "Oh, no! What have I done?"

"Do you think maybe you could remind him that he's deaf?" I asked Caroline, unable to comprehend that I was being condemned because a hearing impaired man had misheard me.

Be less direct, Caroline advised me and Caddy. Be Southern Ladies. Get what you want through smiles, soft tones, subterfuge. Let men think the ideas are theirs.

Caddy and I hooted. Despite her high-heeled pumps, she had the firm, building-vibrating tread of a truck driver; her booming voice echoed in the halls. I was equally, if more subtly, hopeless: no matter how high the hairdresser pouffed my hair, no matter how many times I verbally blessed people's hearts, I was never going to pull off the Southern lady thing. Why couldn't I just speak a little slower, soften the edges of my speech? Caroline suggested.

Caddy and I laughed raucously.

At the end of my second year, I met with the new dean, who was still smoldering because Jason had opposed his appointment to the deanship. He was eager to sympathize with me. I broached the subject of early tenure, the only way I could imagine escaping being browbeaten for the next several years.

"Yes," he said. "Go up now. Next fall, I mean."

"This is only my second year," I said.

"Oh. Well, next year for sure. You just need to realize how great you are!"

\* \* \*

Sometime every summer, I received an evaluation letter signed by Caroline and Jason. The first had been full of praise tempered by cryptic but potentially damaging comments. I was asked to keep in mind the limited backgrounds of many of my students, another veiled request from Jason that I downplay feminist theory. The end of the letter conjectured that it must be difficult for an "accomplished writer" to teach freshman courses, "but you knew you would have to when you took the job." This mystified me, since I'd never made any complaints about teaching freshmen courses.

I wasn't alone in receiving puzzling criticism; Caddy's letter urged her to be less "strident," a word I'd never heard applied to a male faculty member. In fact, on our campus, the same fierceness by men was praised as "passionate."

My letter the next year was even more bewildering. I was thanked for my hard work with students, my publication record, committee work, and long hours spent organizing a writers' workshop. But even the praise sounded weirdly negative. The letter complimented me for working so well with everyone throughout the year despite my "outburst" in the fall.

"My outburst?" I said to Caroline. "Because I disagreed with the grading guide? Isn't that a little infantilizing?"

"You should see what Jason *wanted* to write," Caroline said.

This did not seem good, but I went on clinging to my hope that things would turn out OK because I was harboring a little secret: I had initiated the process to adopt a baby from China. I was well along by the beginning of my third year, when our department held a two-day retreat with the stated intent of completely revamping our freshman program.

I had resolved to just shut up and smile a lot, something I proved constitutionally incapable of. Instead I politely made a case for helping students understand the writing process, examining their work more holistically, and opening up our curriculum to possibilities beyond four-paragraph essays about literature. Jason moaned a few times, but the rest of my colleagues listened carefully, asked intelligent questions, and backed me up.

Then we got down to business. We hacked a few pages off the freshman English reading requirement, added a few more pages to the writing requirement, and decided to deduct two rather than three points for a comma splice. "We've gotten so much done!" everyone chirped. "Can you believe we've made so many changes?"

Though I was frustrated, I went about my business, not wanting to disrupt the surge of goodwill around our department. But disruption was inevitable. One day, Benjy informed me that I would need to spend a week presenting creative writing strategies to his education class. I was teaching five different classes as well as a community workshop to earn money for the adoption. Worn out, rushing all the time, I was just trying to make sure I grabbed the right pile of papers before I zipped off to the next meeting or class. When I told Benjy I couldn't do it, he looked grim.

Caroline noted that I was overwhelmed and exhausted, and she requested a course release to make up for the uncompensated overload I taught every fall. When Jason found out about it, he assumed my release was to enable me to write and he lobbied to make me turn in a weekly quota of pages, as if I wouldn't be productive unless he supervised me despite a record that proved otherwise. Caddy was irritated because she didn't think I deserved a course release as much as she did, since she had a dissertation to finish. Maury rhapsodized about how wonderful it was that I had such an easy semester; now I could write the department's entire accreditation portfolio! And as word got out about my adoption process, Benjy gushed about how great it was that now I had time to prepare for my baby.

Because I was in charge of the accreditation portfolio, I suggested changing our grammar handbook, one that would broaden our scope to meet the standards, which called for more types of writing, more diversity, and more student experience with feedback. Caroline told me to talk to Benjy about it over lunch in the dining hall, but when I mentioned peer feedback, he snapped, "That's a violation of the honor code!" He swept up his tray and stalked off, straight to tell our chairs that I'd brought up an inappropriate topic over lunch and created a "scene."

"Do they always order you around like that?" said a guy from physics. "I'm glad I'm not in your department."

Due to leave for China in late April, I met with the dean the day before. All of his enthusiasm from the previous year had mysteriously evaporated. He had, he told me, worked hard to forgive Jason for trying to block his appointment, and part of his process of Christian forgiveness had meant joining Jason's side. The dean thought I'd better hold off on my tenure application.

"Don't worry about this now!" he told me. "Go to China and get that baby! You've got plenty of other things to think about."

I lay awake all night, consumed by anxiety. Nothing made sense to me. My evaluations ranged from good to excellent, I was doing more service work than any other new colleague, and my publication record was the strongest one on campus. And now I was headed off to China to adopt a baby I wasn't sure I would be able to support.

During the months before I left for China, I'd tried to finish assembling my department's accreditation portfolio. I pled with my colleagues to submit materials as soon as possible, but, overloaded themselves and confused by the educational jargon, no one did.

When I returned home in May, the single parent of a fussy, sick, needy baby, I tackled the portfolio again. Few colleagues had followed directions. I spent hours staring in confusion at pages of standards and syllabi, reading and rereading the somewhat abstract goals that I was supposed to prove that our course materials met: that we helped students develop lifelong habits of reading and writing, promoted learning in their daily lives, and demonstrated through regular practice that reading and writing were interrelated. I had no idea how to demonstrate such intangible things, especially since most of my colleagues hardly taught any writing in their courses.

"This is ridiculous," they had written on their submitted materials. "My whole course does this." I agreed, sympathized, related, shared their frustration, and resented those who were currently bumming around Europe, lying around in lawn chairs reading mystery novels with their phones turned off, and exploring their Jewish roots. Eventually I relieved a little tension by writing my own parody of the standards, with such lines as:

3.1 The program prepares the candidate with knowledge, understanding, and regular practices that will enable the candidates to

3.1.1 Use walking or some equivalent as a major form of ambulation

3.1.2. Use chewing as a primary form of mastication

3.1.3 Include effective swallowing procedures in his/her repertoire of pre-digestive habits

3.1.4 Demonstrate through regular practice how inhaling and exhaling are interrelated

3.1.5 Integrate breathing, eating, and sleeping in his/her daily life-sustaining methodology.

A friend passed this on to the education department. No one cracked a smile.

Silently I fumed and seethed and raged at being stuck in a dark building on sweltering hot afternoons, huddling beside my space heater in long pants and a sweatshirt while air conditioning blasted. At home, my new daughter was so anxious, she wouldn't eat. I missed her. I wondered if she was sleeping. I worried that she was sick on the days that her cry had come out croaky and she'd seemed tired, inconsolable. I was worried about her developmental delays, though they were normal ones for children from orphanages.

And then Snopes, the chair of the education department, called. He wanted me to write a syllabus for a course on educational methodology and teach it in the fall.

"I'm not really qualified to teach that course, and I've already got an overload," I said. "You should talk to my chairs about this."

"I need you to get me the syllabus right away," he said, as if he hadn't heard me.

"Look, I've got a new baby at home and I'm here all day as it is," I said. "Can you please ask my chairs to take care of this?"

"My brother's dying of cancer," Snopes said. "I'd like to be with him, too, but I have work to do. We all make sacrifices."

Finally, I finished the portfolio and turned it in to Snopes's secretary. On my way out, Snopes snagged me. "Hey, I've got this sample methods syllabus for you," he said in his cheerful, blustery way that thinly disguised the fact that he was dispensing orders, not friendly requests. "We'll need yours by next week."

"I can't do it," I said. "I've told you that. I have a new baby. I'm teaching summer classes and I have fall classes to prepare. You need to contact my chairs."

He looked taken aback, as if it were the first time I'd said these things.

"Sorry," I said instantly. "I'm really stressed out. I've got a lot going on and my baby needs me. I'm away from her eight hours a day. I'm just maxed out right now."

Snopes seemed to accept my apology and smoothed things over, but soon after, I received a letter from the dean scolding me for my insubordination to the hardworking education director. And within months, I learned that my department had failed the accreditation though the agency commended my own syllabi and materials.

\*　\*　\*

Only weeks after I became a parent, my father was abruptly diagnosed with cancer and died six weeks later. I arrived in Missouri in time to sit all night in the hospital, listening to his last breaths. Then I took my daughter back to my parents' house to sleep, but I lay awake all night, ragged with shock and loss. In the morning, I checked my e-mail. There was a message from Benjy. He had decided to explain why he would not support my tenure. He felt that I was too overwhelmed by the duties of my job. "And now that you have your beautiful daughter, how will your time be divided?" he had written.

I spent days alternating between writing my father's eulogy and a letter of application: I was going on the job market.

Though I had some interviews, nothing panned out, or maybe I didn't try very hard to find another job, since after a precipitous start to the school year, the thing with feathers had started to sing the tune without the words again. My colleagues and supervisors were generally kind toward an exhausted single mom still reeling from her father's unexpected death. When commuting twenty minutes each way with my daughter to a nearby childcare center proved difficult, I bought a house in town. My co-workers expressed their approval, though Caroline fretted that people would frown on seeing my car in my driveway on Sunday mornings. At any rate, by the end of a fairly calm year during which I learned to juggle my job, motherhood, and my writing, I'd made up my mind: I was going to either go up for tenure or go on the job market in earnest. I submitted my tenure application.

While I was waiting for the decision, Benjy requested that I write the kind of holistic rubric I'd long been advocating so that he could see what it might look like. For weeks I labored over this task, seeking feedback from other colleagues, revising and rethinking it until I was satisfied. When I presented it to Benjy, he barely glanced at it before smilingly informing me that I'd done a great job but he would not vote in favor of incorporating it. Quentin and Caddy philosophically supported the rubric but refused to speak up on my behalf.

I was frustrated. Benjy overheard a snippet of a heated discussion between me, Caddy, and another junior faculty member and went straight to the dean to withdraw his already shaky support of my tenure. Jason had never supported me. Caroline had retired, so she didn't have a vote. Quentin beat his usual hasty retreat from conflict. Maury didn't want to get involved. The dean and the president accepted Benjy and Jason's "majority vote"; after all, their wills left substantial sums to the college.

The rubric no one would support was subsequently adopted and a form of it still exists in the department there today. In fact, recently a young faculty member posted a thank you on Facebook to Caddy and Quentin, who are still there, for their work with her on rubrics, which had helped advance her own career.

"They think you're gay," students said to me. "They think that since you're a single parent, you don't like men." They wrote letters on my behalf and published an editorial in the student newspaper protesting the decision, which I appealed.

"One of the charges against you is that you're a feminist," said the chair of the appeals committee. Quentin, who I'd thought was on my side, brought evidence against me: he had overheard male students in a restroom talking about whether I liked men or not.

I entered the job market after Thanksgiving, past the deadline for most openings. I was still in debt from the adoption, struggling to cover daycare and my mortgage, and terrified about what would become of my daughter and me in such a tight academic job market. But at the eleventh hour, my writing had won some national awards and recognitions that led to a quick tenure-track job offer with a substantial raise in salary.

I was lucky. I had an amazing daughter and a new job, and within two years I'd sold two book manuscripts. I was most surprised that my experience at P.U. didn't silence me or turn me timid; instead, I felt newly empowered to speak up on my own behalf and that of others. Tenure was a breeze at an institution that had a professional system in place that prevented anyone's future from being based on others' whims, although I still sometimes witness disheartening realities that keep women and minorities marginalized. There is still a lot of work to be done.

But I feel lucky every day that even if my hope once led me astray, it also enabled me to survive, that that thing with feathers goes on singing in the chilliest land and on the strongest sea.

# Crossing the Bridge: My Long Road to Tenure

*Robert E Brown*

### Part One: Imagining A Bridge

I spent my first year as an Assistant Professor of English not teaching English. Or anything else.

Like Dante, I had entered a dark wood. Unlike the poet, it wasn't in the middle of my life but the beginning of my career.

I had arrived in L.A. on May 24, 1970, Bob Dylan's birthday, with my wife. We had been married for exactly one week. I was twenty-five and already married twice and divorced once.

Everything was new. My Mexican divorce in Juarez two weeks before my second marriage. The defense of my PhD dissertation at the University of Rochester, the week after returning from Juarez. I intended the dissertation to be a phenomenological reading "response" to *Paterson*, William Carlos Williams's five-volume American epic poem. In fact, it was a rather conventional "close reading," with the ghostly muse of Roland Barthes, Charles Olson, Bucky Fuller, and, pretentiously, Heisenberg's Uncertainty Principle.

I researched the dissertation in the stacks of the University of Rochester library. Then, in the summer of 1969—the moon landing, Woodstock summer—I moved to Boston, rented a fifth-floor walkup on Beacon Hill, wrote the first draft and mailed it off to my adviser in Rochester.

Soon enough, the radio would play Crosby, Still and Nash singing, *Helplessly hoping her harlequin hovers nearby / Awaiting a word.*

I too was awaiting a word from my adviser. A judgment. His letter arrived a month later.

"Your words," he wrote, "are flowers."

Then things turned for the worse. My wife, who had persevered through three winters in Rochester, confessed to having fallen in love with her boss. She told me she had been planning to remain in Boston rather than leave the pretty city for some backwater town and suffer the fate of being the wife of a college professor. I had been counting on an Assistant Professorship at a university in Ontario. I would be going alone.

I began to unravel.

And although there's no opportune time for any such life-altering discoveries (infidelity is up there, believe me), my discovery felt particularly inopportune. It came in December 1969, just a month after I'd been buoyed by the letter from my dissertation adviser. Flowers, indeed. New Jersey obstetrical doctor W.C. Williams was an avid gardener. Flowers make a frequent appearance in his very un-flowery collected poems.

Having received the thumbs-up from my doctoral adviser, I was ready to make the necessary revisions, submit "Walk in the World: A Journey in the Poetic Space of William Carlos Williams," and in the following spring, travel from Boston where I'd written the thing in a five-floor walkup apartment on Revere Street, to Rochester for the triumphant moment that I would hear the lovely, life-altering words, "Congratulations, *Dr.* Brown!"

But by the time I was to hear those words, in May 1970, the arc of my personal narrative was bending low. My center, if I still had one, was no longer holding. A manic-depressive anarchy was loosed on my soul. As for my new title, I was far too small for it. It was a matter not of pride but shame.

*Dear Reader, read on. My story is, as advertised, a comedy, although fringed with sadness. It has been forty-five years since my words were flowers. But all's well that has ended well. Trust me.*

In Dr. Williams's epic, first comes the descent and then the ascent. Radical modernist that he was, when modernist art was all the rage, he made it his mission to tear down the sentimental, Anglophiliac, academic, arcane, T.S. Eliotic, American poetic language of ideas and replace it with a spanking new American language of *things*. (*No ideas but in things*, his motto.)

Poor man! Disappointed, at last, after half a century of his thingy poems, he went all clinical – just as I was to do. Getting on in years by the 1950s, he checked himself into a mental asylum when it seemed to him, that after all he'd innovated, he was to remain unacknowledged. Honors would go to other poets. He died in 1963, and although I was seven years too late to meet him, I got to meet his wife, his grown son and his troubled granddaughter.

But I am getting ahead of myself.

I return now to my own descent which, just as William Carlos Williams's, preceded my ascent. Williams's *Paterson* tells the story of the eponymous Mr. Paterson who is both witness to and cause of the wind and flood and fire that tore through the topography of Paterson, New Jersey and, with the poet's blessing, ravaged the rotting, sentimental, imitative space of American poetics.

My descent, which began with my marital separation, continued in its vividly demonstrable, undiagnosed bipolarity. But before the fall there began weeks of mania centered around my instantaneous burst into a romance on the very day my wife confessed her affair. It was a romance that led to my all-too-soon, imprudent remarriage six months after that painful discovery. More, too, of that story to come.

My new love was Elizabeth. A couple of writers, we quickly became inseparable. My pivot was hardly an altogether unique or surprising turn of events.

At twenty-four, I was the aggrieved victim of an unthinkable betrayal.

Common though such things are, it did not feel like "such things" to me.

From the distance of years and the perspective of my maturity, my first wife was no less aggrieved than I, her "betrayal" neither heartless nor cruel, but the act of conflicted desperation.

I was to see her for the last time before we broke the apartment lease and left for new places to live. Sitting soapy in the bathtub, she told me she loved both her lover and me. I sat on the lip of the tub unable to make sense of it and beginning to dread the future.

I had every reason to do so. For eighteen months, the future would feel dreadful.

FEBRUARY 1970: NEW DIRECTIONS PRESS, MANHATTAN. Things speed up much too fast. I rush into scenes with a passion driven more by mania than boldness.

It is *folie a deux*. Elizabeth, my new thrilling and thrilled, literary, romantic companion and I, barge into literary Modernism's cathedral, New Directions Press, the publishers of Pound, Celine, Paul Bowles, Dylan Thomas, Henry Miller, Marianne Moore, Wallace Stevens, Tennessee Williams and my guy, William Carlos Williams.

I approach the front desk, the typescript of my dissertation in hand, and ask to speak to the famous founding publisher, James McLaughlin. A secretary buzzes his office and he appears. I pitch him my dissertation. He declines, explaining that New Directions is not in the business of publishing literary criticism. Which is not, strictly speaking, the truth. He published Ezra Pound's criticism and a collection by Dr. Williams.

Not only doesn't he show us the door, he dials the poet's widow, Florence (Flossie) Williams, then in her late eighties. I hear him tell her, "I've got a couple of young people you might want to meet." Then, to my surprise, he hands over the phone to me, and I find myself getting directions to 9 Ridge Road, Rutherford, New Jersey, from Flossie Williams. This train, that bus, and the taxi stand. It is as if I am speaking with an aunt, rather than with the woman to whom Williams wrote his lovely late masterpiece, "To Asphodel, That Greeny Flower."

Elizabeth and I were greeted at the door by Mrs. Williams who bade us sit, prepared cups of tea (Liz had the sniffles), and took us for a house tour of one of the citadels of American literature. On the walls were paintings Williams had collected in his days among the modernists in Paris.

After chatting for a while, Flossie seemed to decide these strangers, my girlfriend and I, were OK, and she called through a closed door that it was all right for her granddaughter, Emily, to come out and meet these young people. Mrs. Williams was more than used to young poets showing up at the famous address of the famous poet.

Emily Williams would have been 18 then. One of three Williams granddaughters, she happened to be visiting her grandmother on a short furlough from the Payne-Whitney Clinic, where she was an in-patient under treatment for a schizophrenia that had devolved into suicidal attempts. She warmed to the two of us, the young writers.

I promised we would visit her at the clinic. We did. In her room, on the locked-down ward, the three of us sat on her cot. I brought a guitar and we sang, other patients wandering into the little choir and joining in.

Not long after, Emily visited with us at my parents' apartment (they were away) on Manhattan's Upper East Side. Her father, Dr. William Eric Williams, arrived in the early evening to retrieve her. He brought with him the gift of a book, *A Return to Pagany 1929-1932: The History, Correspondence, and Selections from a Little Magazine.* In its short-lived existence, typical of Twenties Modernism's "littles," the pages of *Pagany* included poems by the era's literary lions, Pound, Dos Passos, Mina Loy, E.E. Cummings (in capital letters, no less), and a great deal of the letters and poems of Williams.

Things went quickly downhill from there.

FEBRUARY 1970: MONMOUTH COLLEGE, WEST LONG BRANCH, NEW JERSEY. I have managed to land a job interview for an assistant professorship. Tough sledding in that year. The jobs for English lit graduate students were scarce—except, that is, for a would-be interdisciplinary/phenomenologist/post-structuralist/postmodernist with shoulder-length hair and a doctoral dissertation in hand. And while I ought to have considered myself extremely fortunate even to land a face-to-face interview, somewhere in the recesses of my amygdala, my reptile brain was seething with resentment and terror.

*I will show you fear in a handful of dust.*

The initial interview with the Chair, and the luncheon, went swimmingly. I was all but a shoo-in, not only for the job but—given the apparent intellectual heft of my soon-to-be-finished dissertation – the Chair believed that I could energize and lead the Humanities Department into the brave new lands of structuralism, post-structuralism, literary Modernism, and into a new academic silo-less world of interdisciplinarity.

After lunch, I was to see the Dean, who would make the final decision.

One would have to be excused from being surprised to hear that sometime during the meeting with the Dean that a candidate would decide to pull from his jacket pocket a harmonica and begin playing a blues. But that is precisely what I did. I don't remember the tune, but the melody lingers on.

History note: This was the era of bad feelings on campus, when student radicals, opposing the war in Vietnam and brandishing Mao's *Little Red Book* railed against corrupted American institutions like universities and their "running-dog" officials, including deans whose offices the rowdy students occupied until the police arrived with batons and tear gas.

To this Dean I looked like that Native American guide in the Western movies, who alone among the Cavalry spoke the Apache language and could negotiate with the savage war party.

Doubtless, one would, further, have to be forgiven for being surprised that a job candidate's rather bizarre improvisatory performance not only didn't lead to his being shown the door, but to the very opposite: a warm and generous handshake followed, in a matter of weeks, by a letter inviting the harp-playing madman to join the English faculty and begin planning to reorganize the Humanities Department.

It was a time of *Off with their heads!* And so here came I—with my long hair, my phenomenological dissertation, my vision of no-more-disciplinary walls, and my blues harp. To the Chair and the Dean, I must have seemed like central casting for the job.

Sure enough, an offer letter arrived from the Chairman of the English Department soon after my astonishingly well-received improvisatory blues performance in the Dean's office.

> Dear Mr. Brown:
>
> *I talked with [the Dean] just now, and we are mailing you a contract letter. The Dean felt that you were the best person we have talked with this year. That made two of us, and, given our merit-raise system, I can't see anything but the brightest future for you at Monmouth College.*
>
> *I think that working here would be exciting for you, because the College and the Department are just in the making, and I want that "making" to take place along the lines which we – all too briefly – laid down in our conversations yesterday.*
>
> *I am going to buy and circulate as "suggesting reading" in the Department copies of some of the books we discussed.*
>
> *Yours is the point of view which I would like to see adopted, not just for the new humanities venture, but for the Department's philosophy in general and the new interdisciplinary major with sociology. . .*

It was the offer of a lifetime. Bright future and all that.

I turned it down.

Within a month, the music I would hear would devolve from an eight-bar blues to a cacophonous siren, and I took to walking around with a piano leg stuffed down my pants to ward off what I imagined could be the imminent attack of an assailant.

I was the Protean man in *Paterson* moved along on his tragic-comic journey. *The descent beckoned.* As Mr. J. Alfred Prufrock's admitted, *In short, I was afraid.*

LATE SUMMER 1970: SAN FERNANDO VALLEY, CALIFORNIA. I'm in my little tan VW, parked on a back road somewhere in the San Fernando Valley. I've been there for I don't know how long. It's late afternoon and I've returned from teaching a class. The class meets twice a week for ninety minutes. It is my only class, and pretty much my only professional responsibility for the summer. My full teaching "load"—that contractual, problematic academic jargon that parses the meaning of "work"—is a single class.

And I am overwhelmed. Not only am I a terrible teacher, I am a fraud. I am filled with an apocalyptic dread at the prospect of September when, as an imposter, I am to be unmasked.

Sitting numbly behind the wheel, I stare like a zombie through the windshield. I fail to take in the pretty, manicured lawns that apron the blood-red bougainvillead homes of the charming hilly neighborhood. What I'm seeing is not the Kandinskyesque patterns Hockneyish SoCal romanticism on a late summer afternoon. What I'm seeing is my death by handgun. Or hanging. (*There! That tree would be perfect!*). Maybe poison. (*Need to check out a book on it, but not from the college library: The librarian would be suspicious.*)

I return to the apartment Elizabeth and I've rented in West Hollywood. Having married at the summer's beginning for the first time (and, as it turned out sadly, for the last and only time), she's begun her new life.

She is filled with anticipation of her future. I do not confide to her that I have no future.

And even if buy a gun and shoot myself in the head, I'd probably only mangle my brain and survive.

Time will cruelly reverse our destinies, Liz's and mine. Four years from that summer, after a summer of headaches, Elizabeth will die of an inoperable brain tumor. Cancer will bore in on her with a surpassing ruthlessness.

But I will have a long and fruitful future.

In the late summer of 1970, I will begin to go to bed earlier and earlier, always wishing never to awaken.

SEPTEMBER 1970: EAST LOS ANGELES, CALIFORNIA STATE UNIVERSITY, 4 P.M. My first class as a contractual, tenure-track, fulltime Assistant Professor. I'm scheduled for two classes. The first begins now: 4 p.m. until 5:30. The second is scheduled for 6 p.m.

I enter the room, carrying copies of my syllabus and distribute them to the students. Did I introduce myself? Perhaps. I don't remember. Why should I? I am planning to kill myself. What I do remember is dismissing the class after brief, fugue-like minutes and heading downstairs to my car. My "plan" was to drive up Route 101 to San Francisco, head for the Golden Gate Bridge and jump.

*The descent beckoned.*

In light traffic, it's about a seven- or eight-hour drive from LA to San Francisco. I never get there. By then, around 400 jumpers had plunged off the bridge, as I would later learn. The vast majority of Golden Gate bridge jumpers prefer to plunge in toward the sparkling city rather than off into the existential seaward nothingness on the other side of the bridge. It was not my night to join them from either side.

I get as far as Santa Maria, then, as now, the agricultural center of a farm-rich valley. Fruits, vegetables and, most memorably, manure.

It smelled like life, not death.

By the time I get to Santa Maria, it's late—midnight, one. The wee hours from a Tom Waits song. It has taken me ages to make it through the yawny traffic sprawl of the LA freeways from East LA to 101.

Thinking about killing myself has tired me out. I'm weary and – oh, yes – *I'm married.* Elizabeth had expected me home hours ago. She'd be dialing the hospitals, police stations, the university, frightened, her thoughts careening. As careless as I was of her feelings (the narcissism of the suicidally inclined), I dial her from a pay telephone outside a Santa Maria convenience store.

*I'm coming home. I'll explain.*

I head back south. Unaided by downhills, the round little VW had a top speed of maybe 85. Which was more or less my speed when I began to be bothered by an inconsiderate bastard with blindingly blue headlights. (*Was that a siren? Did California cars have sirens?*)

I speed up on a downhill as the blue light closed the gap. I'd never owned a car and my driving experience was limited to the three months I had this little brown Volkswagen.

*Pull over! Stop your vehicle!*

Jesus! It's the freaking State Police!

Whatever my explanation for my bizarre manner of operating a motor vehicle—out-of-towner, college professor from Back East, brand new to California—the officer allows me to go on my way with only a pricey speeding ticket and a warning to slow the hell down. (*Oh, those New York city types—they've never had to learn how to drive California freeways. I'll let this idiot college professor off easy with just a summons this time.*)

Dawn is breaking when I arrive home. I fall into the embrace of my tearful, grateful, relieved, puzzled and worried wife. She will accept without understanding, which is, after all, the purest of faith.

LATE SEPTEMBER: EAST L.A. The next day, at my urging, Elizabeth drives to the university and talks the Chairman of the English department into giving me an advance on my paycheck.

I would discover, when I was denied tenure, that the Chairman had come to the reasonable conclusion, in the words of a memo I was given, that whatever ailed me had long been diagnosed by the university as some sort of mental illness.

It would be the perception that knocked me off the tenure-track before I even got off the starting blocks.

## Part Two: The Descent Beckons

In Which The Author Offers A Reflective Chronology Detailing His Circuitous Journey To Tenure.

February 9, 1971: Hollywood, California. Around midnight, still suicidal, I swallow a bottle of valium.
At 6:01 a.m., the Sylmar Valley earthquake topples a hospital. 65 dead. Buildings crumble. The ground shakes with the big shock and aftershocks.
I sleep through it to be shaken awaken by my wife who walks me around the block.

Spring 1971: The 101 Freeway. I fall asleep at the wheel of my car on the way to the Golden Gate Bridge and plow into the weeds without a scratch.
I begin several months of therapy—four days a week with a crewcut former World War II bomber pilot turned M.D. psychoanalyst. He promises not to pink-paper me to a snakepit.

Summer 1971. After being terrified of classrooms, I return to teaching and delight in discussing with students a line in Dr. Williams's famous little enigmatic poem. *So much depends on a red wheel barrow.*

April 1972: London. I travel with Elizabeth through Europe for more than a month. In a London hotel, a telegram comes for me: *you've been terminated.* The faculty union will provide you with an attorney to sue for discrimination.
I can't lose: my lawyer's name is Oliver Wendell Holmes!

December 1972: A Restaurant on Sunset Boulevard. I lose.

June 1973. Academically defrocked nonetheless, I am sent east of Eden to the dreaded "real world," as it would be later mockingly described in the movie, "Ghostbusters." In the real world, things, at first, will not go well.

Summer 1974: Westwood Village, Los Angeles. Hired as a clerk in a toystore, my career in retail will last but a single Saturday morning. The store is packed with moms and their toddlers.
Beginning as a pricing clerk, and unfamiliar with the operations of a pricing gun, I shoot multiple, varying prices onto shelves of toy trucks, Barbie dolls, rubber duckies and board games.
There are complaints.
My career in retail ends before lunch.
Unfit for any job that the Santa Monica Unemployment Bureau has in its files, I collect unemployment. I turn down the single job for which I am

qualified: spending a month in a hospital in a clinical trial on the effects of marijuana.

I demur.

August 1974. During the week of Watergate-disgraced President Richard Nixon's resignation from presidency, I talk the headmaster of an exclusive private school into hiring me.

It proves to be a mistake.

I am unable to control an unruly ninth-grade class. It gets worse. I take the monsters in my Shakespeare class to a West-L.A. movie theater to see "King Lear."

The movie is black and white and far longer than the patience of a class of ninth grade monsters.

When Lear dies, the monsters break into ecstatic cheers and heave their handfuls of candy at the movie screen. Teacher and monsters are ejected.

At the end of the school year, my private-school teaching career is over.

That will prove fortunate.

*The ascent beckons.*

Fall 1974: West Los Angeles. On a 113-degree, statically electric, Santa-Ana windy day of Sunday, October 13, 1974, Elizabeth dies from a brain tumor. She is twenty-eight.

I am twenty-nine. And though it's technically correct, the term "widower" sounds arcane and oddly ridiculous.

Fall 1974 to Spring 1975: San Fernando Valley, California. I join a workshop of published poets and spend a year writing a long poem about grief. It is published by a small press in California.

Thirty years later, I find the little chapbook, *Gathering the Light*, on a shelf in the New York Public Library.

The title will become my Twitter handle.

1974 to 1979: Los Angeles. I land a job editing a bimonthly magazine of "popular history." I begin freelancing articles for magazines.

Soon enough, my expenses are exceeding my income.

One of my editors takes a job in the P.R. Department of a giant oil company. He offers me a job. I go to the dark side.

My wardrobe goes corporate. Wingtip shoes, dark suits, and all manner and color of neckties.

November 1979 to January 1980: Los Angeles. I discover I've a talent for writing speeches.

April 1981 to April 1984: New York City. I hanker for a family, quit my L.A. job, find romance with a good woman in New York, propose marriage (her second, my third). We have a son.

I land a speechwriting job with another big corporation in New York, hate it, get another job a mile away and hate it.

I make an appointment with a career counseling firm. Turns out they're all former nuns. They tell me about the "bird-of-a-feather" theory. Job satisfaction happens when you're with people whose values and tastes are similar to your own.

JUNE 1984: BOSTON. I move to Boston and hire on at a P.R. agency.
It will be a mistake. I am not an agency creature.

NOVEMBER 1985. The agency's president comes to the same conclusion. I am laid off.
It will prove fortunate. Once again I collect unemployment. But not for long.

MARCH 1986. Strolling through downtown Boston, I run into a fellow member of a P.R. trade association I'd joined. She tells me a local college needs someone to teach P.R.

**PART THREE: THE ASCENT BECKONS**

APRIL 1986. I am back in the saddle again (as cowboy Gene Autry used to sing on his T.V. show). Emerson College hires me to teach P.R., a subject considered so off-beat for academia that I am profiled in a business newspaper.

My college salary is half of what I need to support a family. Forget about tenure. Can't afford it.

I accumulate ten consulting jobs to make up the difference.

Can't get tenure anyway. All my writing is for "popular publications," rather than academic journals.

I learn to write in polysyllabic journalese and publish two, second-tier, peer-reviewed articles. Years later, there will be more articles, book chapters and a book.

But it's too late. The articles won't appear until after I'm up for tenure.

I bolt. I take another college teaching job to buy time. *The descent beckons again.*

My marriage falls apart. My job falls apart. I fall apart.

I make an appointment with a psychiatrist. My mantra gets a new name: I am bipolar.

I will not get tenure at this college, either.

I take a one-year, visiting professor position at Boston University.

It goes well. I apply for tenure. I don't get it.

I send out my CV.

SEPTEMBER 1995. SALEM, MASSACHUSETTS. I am fifty. A state college likes my CV. They offer. I accept.
It will be a very good idea.
*The ascent beckons.*

MARCH 4, 1998. BELMONT, MASSACHUSETTS. A letter arrives. It is from the college. I sign for it and slice it open.

> *After reviewing your portfolio, the minutes of our tenure committee, and meeting with you, I am pleased to inform you that I am recommending to the President that you be granted tenure.*
>
> *Sincerely,*
> *Vice President*
> *Academic Affairs*

JULY 1998: BOSTON AND SAN FRANCISCO, CALIFORNIA. I'm on a mission of celebration.

I board a flight to San Francisco. After a night's sleep, I arise early, lace up my running shoes, and jog across the city from Civic Center downtown, and across the city, panting up and down the Tony-Bennett-cable-car hills.
I arrive, at last, at my destination: the Golden Gate Bridge.
Twenty-eight years ago, this was a bridge of death.
But I have not come here to jump off. I am jumping for joy.
Making my way through a rough patch below the bridge of cigarette-butt-and-condom-strewn brambles, I climb dozens of stone steps leading to the bridge. Up there above the bay, in the sunlit clarity, I sprint across. Looking over my shoulder at the hilly, skyscraped city. When I get to the Marin side, I turn around and race back across, this time looking out on the existential nada of the seaward side.
I am lifted with the narrative arc of a long, brambly, vindicating triumph.

### EPILOGUE

We need no classroom or book or professor to inform us that there's no tenure in life. But it took the death of my young wife to drive the message home.
There's a Yeats poem, which I first read and learned to love a half-century ago as student in an English class.

*Speech after long silence; it is right,*
*All other lovers being estranged or dead,*
*Unfriendly lamplight hid under its shade,*
*The curtains drawn upon unfriendly night,*
*That we descant and yet again descant*
*Upon the supreme theme of Art and Song:*
*Bodily decrepitude is wisdom; young*
*We loved each other and were ignorant.*

Among her fellow writers in a San Fernando Valley workshop, Elizabeth had written a number of poems. One of them was about her struggle to find a poetic language. She called it "A Language of Wolves."

I made the title of that poem the title of her collection of her poems, which I published two years after her death.

Elizabeth's life, and her own career as a writer, had hardly begun before it ended.

And so, as the coda to my narrative that arcs from a young man's imagination of a bridge to an older man's crossing it, I shall give her, who never got to cross, the final words.

Looking back on it all, it wasn't procuring tenure that has sustained me, so much as memory and love and the struggle to find a language worthy of the entire comedy.

### A Language of Wolves

I want to write a language of wolves
a catalogue of night
of the hollows in an apple, drying.

I want it to be a gentle word,
Green
the sound of rain
from our bed.

And yet my poems refuse.
They continue coming
from the small, secret boxes
(some have a fresh wood smell
many from ancient heirloom trees
that I'd forgotten.
Boxes that barely wear their names,
Names like
"The Dog That Died"
"A Firefly"

"One Morning")

I keep them locked and scattered in the house, inviting violence.

*A Language of Wolves. Poems by Elizabeth Brown.* Los Angeles, CA: The Laurel Press. 1976.

## Stop Clock, Cover Mirror

*Kathleen Davies*

> Curtains would be drawn and clocks would be stopped at the time of death. Mirrors were covered with crape or veiling to prevent the deceased's spirit from getting trapped in the looking glass.
> —Victorian Funeral Custom

Near Halloween, as my retriever and I were strolling in Woodlawn Cemetery, I stopped to admire a large Catalpa in a section not far from the gate. Its leaves had turned a soft golden yellow, and enough of them had fallen to expose the tree's gnarly branches, its crooked bones. In autumn, it was the spookiest tree in the cemetery. The kind you half expected to snarl like the disgruntled apple trees in *The Wizard of Oz*. Or at least that's what you might half expect in October, the gothiest month of the year. In the fall, I had always loved walking in Woodlawn as a backdrop to teaching "The Legend of Sleepy Hollow," "Young Goodman Brown," Poe's "Raven." But now, it brought me little pleasure. And striking a little too close to home, the wisecracking raven's mantra of *Nevermore!* no longer amused me. These days, nothing much amused me. A few weeks before, the English Department chair, Jim Reaper, had called to inform me that the senior professoriate had voted not to grant me tenure. And today, I was in Woodlawn to ruminate over it.

For five and a half years, Mandy and I had been walking in the cemetery to process the ups and downs of life on the tenure track. Or at least that was what I did there; she was more inclined to chase a groundhog or squirrel. At first, we came to escape the hellhole where the Fates had so carelessly flung us: the postindustrial wasteland of Lima, Ohio, where I had taken a position in English at the Twig, as my colleague friend Nan called it, a branch campus of Big State University (a.k.a. BSU) consisting of three buildings and two trailers, shared with the local community college. Woodlawn was the best place in town, I soon discovered. And that's no exaggeration. The landscape was charming, as much park as Victorian cemetery, with serpentine paths, a bridge, and even a lake. And there were cool statues, too, like the one at the end of the entrance road, where the path branches off: A robed woman with arms extended, offering welcome and blessings to all.

Of course, given the sorry state of the market, I was glad to have any job at all, but not so thrilled to have one at a branch. Although we had the same stiff requirements for tenure as those on the main campus—including a publishable book-length manuscript—we did not receive the same credit or prestige. Worse yet, we were subjected to two sets of reviews: one at the Twig and the other at the English department in Columbus, over ninety miles away. As if it isn't hard enough pleasing folks in your own neck of the woods.

But I had pleased the folks in my neck of the woods—or rather, my little branch of the tree. They had supported my bid for tenure. With enthusiasm no less. It was the review on Main Campus that did me in, presumably because I hadn't finished my book on women's pastoral in American literature. Now that I'd been denied tenure, Woodlawn provided not only solace but an emblem of my doomed career and subaltern status. Mandy and I walked there alone to mull over my demise, my husband, Barry, seldom joining us.

With no reflection from others besides pity or survivor's guilt, I was no longer sure who I was. Metaphorically, my situation was not unlike the old folk custom of stopping the clocks and covering the mirrors when someone dies. Now that the tenure clock had stopped, I was a dead entity as far as the university was concerned, my reflection in the mirror a bit fuzzy, the image of "Professor Davies" now veiled. Of course, respect is the keynote of the custom. Not so in Academe, no siree. No apparent sadness for your passing even, much less respect, at least not by those higher up. The clock stops by default (Do Not Pass Go, Do Not Collect $200), and the mirror is covered by your own abject confusion.

As I stood there looking at the gnarly Catalpa, I thought of Herb McDougal, a colleague friend who had considered suicide after being denied tenure by the English department on Main Campus two years before. The dream of being a professor was so strong in him, was such a consuming part of his identity and self-worth, that losing the prospect of it was almost more than he could bear. Thank God I hadn't invested my own identity or self-worth exclusively in being a professor. In fact, possibly influenced by what I'd seen poor Herb go through (*Alas, poor Yorick!*), the very next day after being "reaped," I resolved not to let it destroy me. In my journal, I wrote, *There is much more to life than all of that. I have a deeper sense of life and of myself inside. I feel that most when I can see myself as just a regular person.* But that didn't mean the tenure denial didn't lower my self-esteem, at least temporarily. If life's tragedies make us stronger, that doesn't happen overnight.

*\*\*\**

Mandy and I walked toward the three Grandfather Pines, as I dubbed them—three very tall pine trees congregating near one of the many crossroads of the path—then paused to gaze at the unadorned headstone coincidentally marked DAVIES. The one that years before made me laugh, nervously, wondering what the fate of my career in Lima would be.

"Kathy, you're so *listless*," I remembered my math colleague Ivo saying when he poked his head in my door the Monday after Reaper's call. He was right. I *was* listless. And despite vitamins, supplements, and a ridiculous amount of sleep, I was still barely dragging myself through the days. I felt like a ghost of my former self.

Nan had rolled her wheel chair up to my office door (a tiny person with enormous glasses, she was severely disabled by rheumatoid arthritis) and, with a pout, sat there in funereal silence. No gossip, no plot summaries, no references to past loves; just a shake of the head. Totally out of character for her normally loquacious self.

"Well, the good news is, I got my Get Out of Jail Free card," I said. The remark wasn't merely facetious. After Reaper's call, there was a part of me that wanted to jump up and down and cheer, "I'm free! I'm free!"

"It's not fair," she whispered.

I dreaded seeing Tim O'Malley and Ken Schmidt, my senior colleagues at the Twig—the only ones eligible to vote at the tenure meeting. (Nan's rank of assistant professor made her ineligible; she had been granted tenure without promotion, a practice the department no longer sanctioned.) The breakdown of the vote—one for, five abstains, the rest against—meant that at least one of them had voted for me (or so I assumed) and at least one had not. I suspected Schmidt to be the one who hadn't.

It was hard not to feel betrayed by that. As the other Americanist at the Twig, he had taken it upon himself to mentor me. He might not have been especially interested in women's lit (his specialty was '60s culture—the Vietnam War, Gonzo journalism, JFK), but he deemed me a good writer, and he had encouraged me to be more aggressive in sending out articles for publication. He had introduced me to his buddy on Main Campus and also to my predecessor, whom I would ask to be an external reader of my book manuscript for the tenure review; invited us to dinner; coached me on how to network. But Schmidt wasn't known for his loyalty, which hinged upon what his English colleagues on Main Campus did. He was desperate for their approval, secretly hoping they'd invite him to join them there, even though such an invitation was rare. After all, he was well published and respected in his field. So I imagined him, sheeplike, baaing a "Nay" along with the majority at my review to show he was one of them.

With O'Malley, whose integrity was solid, I felt I had a special rapport, and I tended to believe he had supported me. The Monday following the review (neither had called me over the weekend), he seemed genuinely sad when he expressed his condolences.

"I'm so sorry," he said. "I really thought we had them. The external reviews were so good." I recalled his excitement when I showed him the letters a few months before.

"Can you tell me what happened at the meeting?" I asked.

"No, we aren't allowed to discuss that."

*Did he look sheepish? Guilty? And why the f\*\*\* was it all so secretive anyway? You'd think it was a god-damned fraternity. Oh wait, it is. . .* (Yes, more women were being hired, especially in the humanities, but academia was—and still is—a boys' club, complete with hazing and blackballing, and the masculine values and culture that accompany that.)[1]

I knew that some senior profs did, in fact, confide what had happened behind closed doors, at least if they felt close to their protégés, but I could see Tim wasn't going to be one of them. I suspected that, as the Twig's assistant dean, he felt obligated to play by the rules.

*Had he been the one who stood by me, or not?*

Schmidt, on the other hand, had come to my door that Monday, trying to sound upbeat.

"Well, it's too bad you didn't make it. But now you need to gear up for finding a new position."

"Yeah, sure," I replied, trying not to cry. I no longer embraced his coaching.

"Have you seen the MLA job list yet?"

*Oh yeah, Ken, right after I got Reaper's call.*

The recommendation letters they wrote for my job search were more telling. I had them sent to a friend at a different institution, who then shared them with me. Tim's was glowing; Ken's lukewarm, damning me with faint praise: "Kathleen is a promising beginning scholar."

A few months later, a conversation between Barry and Tim's wife, Marian, would confirm that Tim had likely stood by me.

"She said Tim was *very* upset about your not getting tenure," Barry relayed. "I don't think he was the one who betrayed you." He looked at me pointedly. No fan of Schmidt, he shared my suspicions that he, not O'Malley, had been the turncoat. After that, I felt more comfortable around Tim, but until then, it was awkward.

\* \* \*

Barking loudly, Mandy chased a squirrel up the hill to the statue of a sad little lady. Not quite full size, she held her hand up to her chin, distraught, tears on the verge of falling, or so I imagined.

Strange, I had cried only once since the denial—the day after Reaper called with the news. And in the years that followed, there would be only a few times when I would actually shed tears over the denial. I would never fully understand why my tear ducts were dry, but exploring cemeteries would become a therapeutic substitute.

I looked over at the four-sided monolith of a nearby monument, not quite phallic, but masculine nonetheless.

*Had the Nathan incident ended up working against me?*

At the end of my second year, Ken had nominated Nathan for the Outstanding Student Award in English. I'd objected. Not only had Nathan already won the award the previous year, he had also crossed a line with me soon after with a letter he left in my campus mailbox. Aggressively misogynist and anti-feminist (he was reacting to a lecture I'd given from feminist critics Gilbert and Gubar on the metaphor of pen as phallus), it was presented as a plan for a novel entitled "City of Meat," an orgy of sexual violence. ("Sex with a knife is the ultimate act of intercourse," he had written.) *Should I be afraid of Nathan?* I wondered when first receiving his letter. After all, I was a woman living alone then, my address printed in the phone book for anyone to see. I decided I could probably take him—he was a little fellow—though who knew what strength a nutcase could muster if driven by rage? After I confronted Nathan with a letter of my own, he replied, not without hostility, "Well, you said you wanted to see my creative writing," suggesting the letter was entirely fictional. There was no indication in the letter that this was the case. The little creep.

After I explained my objection to the English faculty of the Twig, Ken responded with outrage.

"You're *vetoing* us?!" He had been away the year before and had missed getting to nominate Nathan then. He'd be damned if he was going to miss it this time.

"That would never have happened to *me*," Tim said. *Gee, Tim, I wonder why you'd never receive such a letter. Could it be because you're a man?*

Neither he nor Ken wanted to see the letter.

Later, in private, I asked Tim, "What if Nathan had raped me? Would you still give him the award?"

"I don't know," he replied. A staunch civil libertarian, he saw the two issues as separate.

I shuddered to think how I would've fared if I had actually been assaulted by one of my own students. In fact, I was told in confidence that one of our adjuncts, also a woman, had gone through this and received no support at all. How sad that women faculty had to worry about our safety and whether we might be blamed for an attack against us.

As for the award, we ended up making a compromise with Nathan sharing the award with another student, and I sought to repair any damage done. And all seemed well. The following year, Ken stepped up his mentoring of me, often stopping by my office to chat, helping me make connections, offering encouragement and advice.

No, I didn't honestly think either of the guys held a grudge against me for the Nathan incident, at least not enough to vote against me.

But what did one or even two votes matter anyway? Not much.

\* \* \*

Mandy and I followed the path near the front of the cemetery, past a bronze woman in chiton reading a tablet, its words reminding me of poor Herb (*Each departed friend is a magnet that attracts us to the next world*); continued on to walk between the Thompson and McCauley mausoleums built into the hills on either side, facing each other (*Yea, though I walk through the valley of the shadow of death...*); hung a left at Gros-Maire, which squatted on a small island at a crux of pathways.

*Was it unfair, as Nan had said?*

It was true I hadn't finished the book on time, but I had submitted a manuscript over three hundred pages long. And if someone like John Owens, who had accomplished far less than I, could be granted tenure simply because he was from Yale and had connections, then what did fairness even mean? (Later, as John's case moved up the chain of command, the Dean of Arts & Science would reverse the department's pass.)

My book, entitled *The Green Letter: A Tradition of Women's Pastoral*, might not have been cutting edge, but it was solid and important. In it, I argued that many women writers appropriated natural tropes and pastoral conventions to claim literary power. A key strategy to that end was to rework the Machine in the Garden, the classic paradigm delineated by Leo Marx, into the Phallus in the Garden, which was used subversively to critique and exclude male characters who exhibited dominance or aggression. The book extended my dissertation, which covered several American women's 20$^{th}$-century novels, into the 19$^{th}$ century and included poetry as well as fiction. No doubt the scope was too ambitious for the time I had. But shouldn't breadth and ambition count for something? Be rewarded? Perhaps even warrant special consideration? Especially since the research for it had to be done old style with handwritten interlibrary loan requests and trips down to the library on Main Campus. Unfortunately, the part I hadn't finished—the late 19$^{th}$-century literature—left a gap, which meant I couldn't simply declare the book finished when it was time to submit the manuscript for the tenure review.

Nevertheless, my scholarship received positive feedback from various quarters. But as I discovered during my autopsy report with Reaper, my English colleagues on Main Campus dismissed nearly all of it. That my chapter on Margaret Fuller was selected to be presented at the Modern Language Association Convention—normally a coup, especially for junior faculty—hadn't meant much to them. Nor had the other fifteen presentations I'd given over the years. Or the talks to the community. Or the articles I'd published.

Five of the six reviews of the book from peers outside of BSU were glowing, yet they were written off completely with flimsy excuses and half-assed assumptions. (*The most famous one probably hadn't bothered to read the whole manuscript; that one used to teach on the Lima campus and was therefore biased*, etc.) Ah, but the negative one was latched onto, its political agenda completely overlooked. (Fearing that it would offend men, my critic clearly wanted to distance herself, ecofemism, and ecological literary criticism from the subversive ways in which my authors used the pastoral to punish or exclude aggressive male characters.) As far as I could see, requiring external reviews was a sham, used only to support hidden agendas while giving the appearance of objectivity and fairness.

Even though I hadn't finished the book, seven university presses—one unsolicited—had expressed interest in publishing it when it was finished. Yet six were dismissed as "second tier" because they were located in the South. Only a year earlier, this had been adequate for another regional campus colleague to get tenure. The more prestigious University of Illinois Press was blown off as well.

Still, the fact remained: *I hadn't finished the book.*

And I was running out of steam.

All that work. All that effort and sacrifice. And I was going to lose my job anyway.

* * *

In the cemetery, we headed toward the holding vault, where they used to keep the bodies awaiting burial in winter. On its top were the heads of two snarling lions, flanking the carving of a holly wreath.

The lions made me think of Jim Reaper. Tall, gaunt, morose, Reaper was a figure to be reckoned with. He had all the power to steer the course of my fate, and I was pretty sure he held a grudge against me, which would explain the bias against me. Certainly, he and I had had a number of grim encounters.

It all began with the *Beloved* incident.

I thought back to my second year and the workshop I'd attended featuring Reaper's unintentionally disturbing paper on the novel. Nan had joined me, and on the trip down in her van, we had a high old time critiquing the hell out of Reaper's paper.

"He makes his desire to 'enter' and 'penetrate' the novel sound like a rape fantasy," I'd scoffed.

To which Nan had tittered with glee. She despised Reaper's smugness, along with that of most of our colleagues on Main Campus, almost as much as I did. Because we were regional faculty, they assumed themselves to be superior to us.

"And there's something not quite right about the way he shifts gears," I added, groping my way toward understanding, as I do. "He's stuck in a subject-object dichotomy, then seems to want to shift toward a paradigm of multiplicity but without quite recognizing what he's doing, which seems pretty lame for a theorist."

"Oh, that's *good*," Nan gloated. "We're going to impress the hell out of them."

"Well, I don't think we should mention the rape part," I replied.

And of course we didn't. But silly us for thinking they wanted to be impressed by our keen intellect.

During the workshop, I watched aghast as one feminist after another kowtowed to Reaper, almost fawningly. Not one alluded to his rapist mentality, not even in subtle, face-saving terms. Playing the grande dame, Marcy Longaberger had even patted Reaper on the back, saying perhaps Annie, his wife, had been a positive influence on his awareness of being a male reader. *Seriously?* Nan and I exchanged surreptitious glances. *Why were they were handling him with kid gloves?* What did they know that we didn't?

Afterward, the sole black woman in the department—recently recruited from a nearby college and no doubt very astute about workplace politics—walked up to us and said, in the most congenial way, "My, you two sure have a lot to say! I'll have to get you to read my work sometime." But her eyes relayed the deeper message: *This is a game you need to learn how to play if you're going to survive.* It was then I realized my faux pas: What was expected was not my participation—astute or otherwise—but my silence.

A year later, Reaper became departmental chair.

When I read the announcement, the hair on the back of my neck stood up. The changing of the guard is the sort of shift that wrecks careers. Rules get changed, antes are upped, loyalties shift. In Reaper's case, this meant reviews not only at the fourth and sixth years but annually with a chapter- or article-length writing sample. Instead of the publishable manuscript by the sixth, a contract lined up. Yes, the changing of the guard was a common factor in questionable denials.

This was my third year on the track, and so quite hastily, I had to face my third-year review with Reaper and the deceptively cute Lil Appledumpling, who served as the departmental pit bull. *Grim, grim, grim.* And maybe it wouldn't have been, if I had only been more strategic and given them the published article on Hurston that everyone liked, or the book's chapter based on it, as a sample to discuss. Something tried and true, polished. But *noooo*, I had to give the latest chapter I'd been working on and felt excited about, the one that explained the key trope of the green letter, hoping not only to impress them but also to get some useful feedback. So *not* shrewd.

Lew Brooks, chair of the P&T committee and a noted creative writer, was impressed with it, actually. Outside of Reaper's office, he had met me with friendly encouragement.

"I'm a little nervous," I confided. Probably not the best thing to say.

"Oh, I'm sure it will go well, Kathy," he said as he ushered me into Reaper's office.

But once he saw which way the wind blew during the meeting, Lew turned cool toward me forever after.

"Well, I want to know what you mean by 'women,'" Lil taunted right off the bat. (I'll bet they rue the day they recruited her.) "Surely there were women of color writing about nature during the early nineteenth century."

But for the most part, there weren't. Though the slave poet Phillis Wheatley had employed the pastoral mode in some subversive ways, she did not appropriate it as a woman. Obviously, very few women of color had either the literacy or the leisure to write, much less the privilege to publish, in the pre-Civil War era.

"How do you define 'pastoral'?" Reaper next interrogated. A legitimate enough question, of course, but asked in such a belligerent manner, it made me feel like I was defending my dissertation all over again (although my profs had been a lot more respectful). Instead, he could have treated me like a colleague and used my explanation in the chapter as a springboard for discussing it. In his official write up of the review, Reaper managed to make it sound as if I were an imbecile who didn't understand her own topic.

*If only I were better on my feet. If only. If only. If only....*

If only I didn't suck at promoting myself and my work.

And then, there was the mistake I'd made of offering a compliment that he ended up using against me. It came before the debriefing of my fourth-year review, when Reaper said he needed to finish putting away some files before we began.

"That's impressive," I'd said in an effort to be friendly. "I should be as organized as you are!"

Next thing I knew, in his summary letter for my file, he noted that I was "disorganized."

Yet *he* was the one who managed to leave out *half* of my student evaluations—the best ones, too—for the fourth-year review. If that didn't prove he was out to get me, I didn't know what did. My dean in Lima advised me to point out the error in a rebuttal. Surely he held that against me, right? A more ethical person—like O'Malley, for instance, or myself with students—would have bent over backward to avoid letting negative bias interfere with evaluation. Reaper seemed to have no such inclination, which is what made him so dangerous.

Across the path was the Brice monument—rumored to have been designed by Saint-Gaudens, complete with lions' feet on the mourning benches, echoing the leonine motif of the holding vault. How many times over the years had I stood in front of it, soaking in the comfort and encouragement of the wise words carved into it?

*Let not your heart be troubled.*
*Neither let it be afraid.*

Yet I should have been more afraid of Reaper.

\* \* \*

It seemed unfair that regional faculty had to juggle two campuses. That our fate was decided by people ninety miles away, few knowing us or our work first hand.

Mandy and I walked up the steps of Mitchell-Baxter to see its lovely stained glass windows of the Three Graces, so beautiful they might have been designed by Louis Comfort Tiffany himself. In muted tones of blue and mauve, the three were joyful in one window, pensive in the other.

When Mandy and I first started coming to the cemetery, I had a fantasy of Woodlawn as a commune. Instead of cabins, little stone houses. I'd picture myself with a basket looped over my arm, walking on the path to Sunny's, or Ruthie's, or Joe's. I'd pause at their doors, hand each a loaf of zucchini bread, chat about politics or the weather, compare notes on how the fish were biting at the lake that week. I'd admire their tomato plants—*Oh yeah, that organic fertilizer is some good shit, man. Nothing like a graveyard for fertile soil.* Invite them to drop by my place later.

I was thinking about community and wondering how I'd fit in—not so much at the Twig, where marginality seemed to bind us in a kind of congenial cynicism, as on Main Campus, Ivory Tower Proper. Did my colleagues there truly see me as one of them?

My first encounter led me to think maybe they did.

"Why, you're one of us. You should be *here*!" exclaimed a fiction writer after I introduced myself at the departmental meeting in Columbus that kicked off my first quarter. (Onlookers appeared dubious.) Then she handed me her card, extending an invitation to call her when I was in town. I was flattered until I realized that, if she really considered Twig faculty equal, the remark wouldn't have been made at all.

A far worse encounter was with Patricia Smiley, a sour puss if I ever saw one, whom I met at the departmental party hosted in Columbus by Maury Singer, the chair who had hired me and would later be replaced by Reaper.

"Where are you from, and what is your specialty?" she asked me.

"I'm from the Lima Campus—." Before I could finish answering her, she abruptly cut me off.

"Well, that doesn't mean you don't have a specialty."

My immediate response was an unintelligible stutter.

Did she really think that uttering such an incredibly patronizing remark was being supportive? By God, I thought she did.

Being a woman in Academe even in the 1990s—no, we hadn't come all that far, Baby—was like being an immigrant. Being a woman from the Twig doubly—almost literally—so. And Smiley seemed like one of those accomplished assimilators who turn against the newcomers.[2]

Meeting Lydia Miserovsky (one of those dubious onlookers) was a better experience.

"So you're from Indiana?" she asked. "Did you work with Susan Gubar?" Famous for co-authoring the groundbreaking study *The Madwoman in the Attic*, Gubar was known by every feminist critic.[3]

"She was on my dissertation committee. Such a brilliant woman."

"Yes, she is. I took an NEH seminar with her several years ago."

Great, I remembered thinking, this is the stuff connections are made of. How ironic that my connection to Gubar would only end up biting me in the butt.

Since women's lit was my specialty, it was important to connect to the feminists on Main Campus. In hopes I could establish rapport with them, Maury had advised me to join their discussion group. I had belonged to a similar group in grad school, but the dynamic was different in this group, as I discovered at my first meeting.

After I posed a question about an article we read on post-colonial feminism—an approach I adopted from my group at IU—Longaberger went into lecture mode. Was she trying to impress the grad students there?

Afterward, she looked at me and asked, "Does that answer your question?"

I might as well have been a grad student myself.

Marcy liked to show off her knowledge of "theory," and I noticed that she and the others deferred to my good buddy Patricia Smiley, who was clearly the most fluent in pomo speak. They rattled off the latest postmodern jargon about the glories of the "destabilization of identity" and the "decentering of the unified subject." (Unabridged bullshit version: the *decentering of the humanist subject consequent upon the postmodernist critique of subjectivity*.) They talked about "problematizing" women (but never men, why was that?) without batting an eye or cracking the subtlest smile of irony. It was as if, like immigrants, they were over eager to prove their mastery of the language of the dominant culture. Just thinking about it made me feel destabilized and decentered.

For several years, I faithfully attended the quarterly meetings in Columbus, hoping to establish myself in this community. Of the bunch, Lydia extended herself to me the most, occasionally asking how things were going, but my connections to the department feminists were tenuous at best. None seemed especially interested in my work or very invested in me or my future at BSU.

Had a single one voted on my behalf? I doubted it, and it hurt that, ultimately, I got so little support from them. Was I wrong to have expected it?

Had any of them felt the slightest twinge of guilt?

I would gain some insight into this nearly a decade later at a tribute for Susan Gubar at IU, when I spoke with a woman who started teaching at the Twig my last year there. Then, she had kept her distance—after the denial, you would've thought I was radioactive—but now, at our alma mater, she was more open.

"I believe you got the shaft," she said bluntly.

"Really?" I was surprised at her candor. "I felt let down by the feminists on Main Campus," I confided.

"I think they felt bad about what happened to you, Kathy," she said. "So they made more of an effort with me and some other women." At least my demise ended up helping others.

Although the revelation came ten years after the fact, it was nonetheless validating.

\* \* \*

The vibrant colors of the autumn leaves reflected on the lake along Woodlawn's back border. I breathed in the rich, spicy fragrance of the leaves nearby. How ironic that decay smelled so sweet.

And how ridiculous that my teaching was judged by how well I taught on Main Campus. Because my colleagues in Columbus couldn't be bothered to make one trip up to Lima to observe my teaching at the Twig, I had to teach three courses down there for an entire quarter, driving 180 miles' round trip twice a week for ten weeks—time better spent doing research— so they could evaluate my teaching of *their* students on *their* campus. Never mind that my students were different from theirs, with different needs; that many were older, had children and jobs; had special challenges, including poverty, to deal with; that many were the first in their families or among their friends to attend college, for which they were sometimes given a hard time. Because of the looming deadline for the fourth-year review, I had to have them observe me within the first two weeks of classes, just I was getting acquainted with the students. Ironically, Lew harassed me about getting these in earlier until I reminded him of the circumstances.

Lydia and Marcy wrote very positive evaluations of my special topics course, "Cultural Intersections." Marcy said my way of conducting the discussion was "magical," among the best she'd seen anywhere. But then the fiasco: Some of the good students in the class were put out with one who didn't do the readings and blamed me for it, resulting in the lowest student evaluation scores of my career. What was I supposed to do, visit the girl's dorm room and stand over her like a fascist nun with a ruler poised to thwamp her knuckles every time she looked up from the page? When I tried to address this for the tenure review, Smiley said I was "blaming the students" for my failure. I was certain this single course had loomed disproportionately large in the overall evaluation of my teaching as merely "good."

My students and colleagues at the Twig saw my teaching differently. On our campus, I had earned a reputation for being an excellent teacher, and students were eager to take my classes. The dean had even asked me to coach a colleague in sociology who had wretched student evaluations. Twice I had been nominated for the Twig's Outstanding Teacher Award. Twice also (and a third time, later) I had been invited to the University-Wide Salute to Undergraduate Achievement Banquet. Hadn't I proven that my teaching was better than "good"?

I wonder if they cared much about teaching anyway. They seemed to use whatever they could—even downplaying your successes—to justify denying you tenure if that was what they'd decided they wanted to do.

One of the secrets of my popularity was that I didn't put on airs. I never went to the "dark side," as I'd seen so many do, becoming that haughty, ego-inflated caricature of professorial erudition that students loathed and I found repugnant. I didn't feel comfortable cultivating an aura of omniscience and authority that would distance me from students. I didn't fit the mold. I was there to inspire and encourage my students, change their lives even, or at least have a positive impact. That's why I created special topics courses like "Rebels" and "Diving Deep & Surfacing." Yet all of this may have worked against me, too.

I loved teaching, and I loved my students. I'd been doing it for almost twenty years. It was my calling. I didn't see myself embarking on a new career. But how hard would it be to find another position? Would I end up like Herb—teaching a gazillion courses as an adjunct for poverty wages the rest of my life?

* * *

Suddenly, I felt the urge to visit Mary Baker. Her headstone belonged to a group of markers that had been moved from an old churchyard in town—no doubt without the bodies—and was likely all that remained of her. Since the first time I deciphered its florid script scratched into the sandstone, I'd been haunted by Mary's epitaph.

*In*
*Memory of*
*Mary Baker*
*who died*
*Aug. 2, 1838*
*Aged 29 years, 6 mo.*
Her languishing head is at rest,
Its achings and thinkings are o'er,
This quiet immoveable breast
Is heaved by affliction no more.

Sometimes, I felt afflicted, driven half mad by the extraordinary demands and pressures of the tenure track, along with the challenges of doing feminist literary criticism in the 1990s. This was where my connection to Susan Gubar ended up backfiring. *The Madwoman in the Attic* had been my inspiration for *The Green Letter*. I had adapted Gilbert and Gubar's theory—that some nineteenth-century women writers created madwomen or some other subversive alter ego to vent the anger they dare not voice directly in a patriarchal society—to argue that my authors subversively employed nature and pastoral conventions to the same end. But a few years after its publication, *Madwoman* had been trashed. Not merely criticized for its shortcomings, which was to be expected, but *trashed*, and by other feminist critics, the sell outs (or so I thought) who had climbed aboard the post-structuralist bandwagon. Their sins? Using the word "women" generically (as if it wasn't understood that they were referring to the nineteenth-century

English and American white women authors they explored in the book), along with believing that authors were relevant to the texts they wrote.[4]

With the annihilation of *Madwoman*, my foundation had been yanked out from under me. Now it was impossible to discuss "women's" literary traditions and strategies without setting oneself up for attack, at least in some circles. If I had been hired by a different sort of department—one where Gilbert and Gubar's work was still respected—this wouldn't have been an issue. After all, both critics continued to build stellar careers, publishing numerous books and articles, receiving awards and much deserved recognition for their contributions.[5] But the English Department at BSU was interested in building their reputation, which meant they needed to be a "theory" department. Constantly worrying about their criticism of my approach was distracting and made writing difficult. But what could I have done? Gut my dissertation entirely and start from scratch? Seeing the writing on the wall, Lydia had gone one step further: she switched fields entirely. Just before my fourth-year review she confessed, "After what happened to Gilbert and Gubar, I bagged literature and went into film studies." It was certainly too late for me to do that.

I had no one to turn to for advice. Nan wasn't in my field, nor was she an active scholar. As for feminist criticism, Schmidt wasn't an expert in my field either. My dissertation director had moved to Germany soon after I started it. Her co-director, who really hadn't been all that helpful, had died my first year in Lima. I didn't feel comfortable consulting Gubar about the criticism of her approach. Nor was it wise to reveal vulnerability to my feminist colleagues on the main campus. Offers of help from feminist critics outside of BSU would come belatedly, right before the tenure review and then after the denial.

The issue with *Madwoman* was pivotal for at least one of my readers at BSU. Sarah Bighead, a 19th-century American scholar and current golden girl of the department, questioned my acceptance of Gilbert and Gubar's thesis, which she felt had been "disproven" (as if literary theories had criteria equal to scientific ones). Conversely, Beatrice Flowers, whose work I had little respect for, had asked me to provide her with a reading list of feminist criticism so she could *begin* to understand the chapter I'd given her to read. Comments relayed during the autopsy with Reaper confirmed the group's blind reliance on these two figures, which explained the extraordinary reversal of nearly unanimous support at the fourth-year review, to nearly unanimous *dis*approval at the sixth.

Several stones over from Mary, I noticed the stern visage of Lamenta, carved bas relief into a white marble headstone with a rounded top. She reminded me of Patricia Smiley. The disapproval of both seemed palpable.

\* \* \*

"Farewell, Mary."

I waved goodbye to her, gave Lamenta a nod.

Mandy and I continued along the path overlooking an open field designated for future plots. We walked toward the Michaels monument—my favorite—an Art Deco mausoleum, complete with sun disc and vulture's wings over the doorway and sphinxes guarding its inhabitants. A peculiar appropriation of Egyptian Revival architecture for a family of Jewish émigrés from Germany, or so it seemed to me.[6] Below was the meadow where Mandy loved chasing groundhogs. Ahead, the Taylor pyramid with its coat of arms, another quirky amalgam of cultures.

Soon, I would begin prepping another special topics course for winter quarter—"The Quest"—designed as much for me and my ghostly self as for students who might also wish to explore identity issues. I was hoping with this I might rend the veil, uncover the mirror and possibly with an *Abracadabra!* meet my new self, or rather my old "truer" self, whatever that might be, and get back on the right path.

When we passed the sphinxes, I could swear they smirked.

Should I appeal the decision? I briefly considered the option but was so exhausted from the process and my demise, I knew I didn't have it in me. Nor did I feel confident in a favorable outcome. After all, I hadn't finished the book. A couple of people had suggested that BSU could have given me an extension to finish it if they'd really wanted to. And perhaps still would, especially if the University of Illinois Press came through with an advance contract (which it did that December). But I didn't think the people at BSU were interested in that. I felt they were done with me.

In less than a week, it would be All Soul's Day, when Catholics pray for the dead, especially those who, like me, languished in Purgatory. I would have to remember to pray for myself.

---

Notes

[1] Between 1980 and 2000, the period that followed Title IX and coincides with the period I was immersed in academia, the number of tenured males was increasing 30% faster than the number of tenured females, despite the influx of women at that time (data from the Association of American University Professors, as reported in Jane Roland Martin's *Coming of Age in Academe: Rekindling Women's Hopes and Reforming the Academy* (New York: Routledge UP, 2000), p. xi). It was only in the late 1990s that BSU finally tenured a woman who had taken maternity leave while on the track.

Sadly, the status of women in academia has not improved much in the years since. In her 2014 "The Status of Women in Academia," Rachel Croson reports that "Women are less likely to be granted tenure in every field" (see https://awf.wustl.edu/wp-content/uploads/ 2014/04/crosonwashugendertalk.pdf). For a specific example, Eric Anthony Grollman quoted a study of tenure rates at the University of Southern California in his 2013 article, "On Racist and Sexist Discrimination in Academia": "Since 1998, 92% of white males who were considered for tenure got it [whereas] only 55% percent of women and minority candidates were granted tenure" (in *Conditionally Accepted: A Space for Scholars on the Margins of Academia,* 9-2-13 (see http://conditionallyaccepted.com/2013/09/02/racism-sexism-academia/). Suggesting that survival tips are still very much necessary, in her recent blog, *The Professor Is In,* former professor Karen Kelsky offers advice to women who aspire to succeed in academic settings, along with support for those who wish to leave academia as she did (see http://theprofessorisin.com).

As for the masculine culture, Martin reports that academic women are inherently pressured to identify against themselves and other women, a situation that makes them feel like "immigrants" in a foreign culture. And Scott Jaschik's 2008 *Inside Higher Ed* article, "'Quiet Desperation' of Academic Women," chronicles the deep frustration women in academia experience due to discriminatory practices and values (see https://www.insidehighered.com).

[2] Jane Roland Martin, *Coming of Age in Academe: Rekindling Women's Hope and Reforming the Academy* (New York: Routledge, 2000).

[3] Sandra M. Gilbert and Susan Gubar, *The Madwoman in the Attic: The Woman Writer and the Nineteenth-Century Literary Imagination* (New Haven: Yale, 1979).

[4] See Toril Moi, *Sexual/Textual Politics: Feminist Literary Theory* (London: Methune, 1985); Jane Gallop, Marianne Hirsch, and Nancy K. Miller, "Criticizing Feminist Criticism," *Conflicts in Feminism,* ed. Marianne Hirsch and Evelyn Fox Keller (New York: Routledge, 1990); Janet Todd, *Feminist Literary History* (New York: Routledge, 1988); and Susan Gubar, *Critical Condition: Feminism at the Turn of the Century* (New York: Columbia, 2000).

[5] Since *Madwoman,* Gubar has published eighteen books, with another on the way in 2016. Two were written after her diagnosis in 2008 of stage 4 ovarian cancer. The influence of *Madwoman* is celebrated in *Gilbert and Gubar's Madwoman in the Attic after Thirty Years,* Ed. Annette R. Federico (Columbia: U of Missouri), published in 2009.

[6] Peculiar or not, the appropriation is not uncommon, according to Diana Muir Appelbaum in "Jewish Identity and Egyptian Revival Architecture," *Journal of Jewish Identities* 5.2 (July 2012): 1-25 (readily available at <https://independent.academic.edu/DianaMuirAppelbaum>).

# Arbitrary & Capricious

## *Michaela Valentine*

*To tenure or not to tenure?* used to be the question. Now, more often than not, it is a foregone conclusion resting squarely on the side of *not*. So what is the social context such that bright, ambitious, talented teachers, especially with PhD's in hand, are only perfunctory candidates for Assistant Professor status but become permanent adjuncts instead? A wide swath of blame exists with a full panoply of accomplices. College administrations with their Boards of Trustees backing them are set on union busting and obliterating tenure altogether. Oblivious/acquiescent/and-or jealous full-time tenured faculty have lost sight of the privilege, agency, and sovereignty that tenure affords and have permitted the slow erosion of the profession into designated and powerless castes. My personal denial-of-tenure story involves all of the above.

Picture a small, community college in Central New Jersey in 2002 that I will call Oceanic Community College. One year out of graduate school, I was hired from a huge pool of applicants to fill a tenure-track vacancy in the English Department, one that had languished for some seven years during which time legions of part-timers were hired at sub-standard wages without benefits or contracts to keep the majority of the classes going. I had attended a well-known and reputable College in Central Virginia and had earned a PhD in American Studies (History & English). Thanks to numerous research grants, I was able to research my dissertation subject at major academic libraries like Yale, Harvard, and Fisk, at the Library of Congress, and I completed my dissertation with a generous grant from the Radcliffe Institute for research on women. I had also received a dissertation grant from my College and numerous research grants. Once I was ABD, thanks to the wonderful English Department at the College where I was enrolled, I was allowed to teach classes in American & African-American Literature all the way up to 400-level courses and to compete for the coveted special topics senior seminars. I had also taught in an intensive summer learning experience meant to assist inner city and minority students and to help ensure their adaptation and success after they had been admitted to the college on a provisional basis. In short, I was more than qualified for the position for which I was selected, and I came to my new job with all the energy, enthusiasm, intelligence, and skill I had needed to earn my advanced degree. I also had acquired some fifteen years of teaching experience at both community and four-year colleges.

Add to the picture of this small but vibrant community college where I was hired a lively faculty union now face-to-face with a new college

President. Dr. Learson in his inaugural address claimed he wanted to make Oceanic the "Harvard of community colleges." In fact, he nearly destroyed its overall integrity and commitment to its students in favor of other goals supported by its Board of Trustees and the elected Board of County Freeholders. This sleight-of-hand was made possible in part by special circumstances that existed in New Jersey at the time of my hire. Unlike most of its neighboring states, New Jersey had abolished the State Department of Higher Education under a recent Republican administration. It was replaced with the Council of College Presidents that had absolute authority over how education dollars were allocated. Add to this anomaly that the hiring committee for this new College President was headed up by two Oceanic faculty members—Jane Hubris and Rick Stagnant—both tenured professors, with MA degrees only, who simultaneously craved the kinds of promotions that normally come with the possession of PhD's and publications, neither of which they could claim. It was later revealed that Dr. Learson, the Presidential candidate they found and supported, had been forced to resign from his previous Presidency at a college in Pennsylvania, having among other offenses, a sexual harassment charge against him by a minority woman at his college and under his employ. This intentionally corrupt vetting process was a complete perversion of the committee's charge to find the best candidate for the job of President of OCC. In the eyes of Hubris and Stagnant, Jack Learson was just such a man to assist in their climb to new levels of unearned authority and position; indeed, one was predictably elevated from faculty member to assistant to the President. Sadly, this subversive intent went largely unnoticed by the rest of the faculty, who did not know of Learson's past but should have. During this tempestuous time in higher education, according to the *Chronicle of Higher Education*, which few of them read, tenure and unions were under continual assault across the entire U.S.

*To sign or not to sign?* was the question at hand during my third year at Oceanic Community College. A petition to the College President on behalf of the English Department was put before me alleging that Dr. Learson had threatened the student editors of the *Oceanic Chronicle* in a private session after they initiated an inquiry into a matter involving a suspicious awarding of a contract by the College. The undersigned demanded that he desist his assault on the First Amendment and the student editors' prerogative to freedom of inquiry. Of course I signed. I support the important principle of freedom of the press, and, more importantly, two of the editors were students in my advanced composition class. Frankly, it never occurred to me not to sign. At the very least, I would be abdicating personal responsibility as a tax-paying citizen of Oceanic County. More importantly, I would have been ignoring my responsibility to my students to support them in their legitimate educational endeavors. Yes, I was the only untenured member of the English Department to sign the document, but in the best of all possible worlds that correct choice should not be misconstrued as a test of tenure-worthiness, which it quickly became, though never in point of fact.

My previous experiences with community colleges were wholly positive, beginning in the mid-1980s when I returned to the West Coast city where I grew up in order to adjunct in the English Department of River Falls Community College. At the time, I had only a Master of Arts degree from a Northeastern State University and four years of teaching experience at two different four-year colleges in New England. Many of my colleagues at RFCC were former Peace Corps volunteers or liberal advocates of the community college mission to provide an affordable college education for everyone who desired it. Although I was not a tenure-track hire because I lacked a terminal degree, I was treated fairly and collegially. The full-time faculty union had even negotiated the following: that every third quarter of teaching (we were on the quarter system then), adjuncts would receive full benefits for that quarter. What this arbitration meant was that we could get our dental and medical needs taken care and paid for at least once during the academic year. It was a welcomed and unexpected benefit. Also during my four years at RFCC, when full-time faculty members were granted a one-time 7% raise by the Washington State Legislature, they voted to pass it on to the long-term adjuncts instead of themselves. It was a public admission on their part that the adjunct system was an unjust caste that they disavowed in the most fundamental sense of pay equity.

I was favorably disposed toward RFCC even before I applied to teach there. Almost every member of my family, including my parents, had taken classes there or graduated with an AA or AS degree that lead either to gainful employment or to matriculation into a four-year college. My mom, a single mother of nine, was able to earn an AS degree to become a case worker in a special program created by the Department of Health and Human Services to assist indigent mothers with minor children. My father, who was AWOL from the Army due to untreated schizophrenia, earned a mechanical engineering degree sufficient for employment with the County Engineers. My oldest sister earned an AA degree and went on to earn a BS and an MSW. She became an elementary school Social Worker while she and her husband raised a daughter who went on to earn an MSW like her mother. My twin sisters both earned B.A. degrees after attending RFCC. One became a freelance artist who uses her knowledge of anthropology to include indigenous peoples and their customs in photography, watercolors, and oils. The other also earned an AA degree and then a BA in English. She became a poet and the owner of an artsy bridal boutique. She has designed jewelry for three Miss Connecticuts and a member of the Supremes, among many others. A younger sister, having earned an AA degree, went on to a four-year college in Western Washington and became both a successful member of a building department, an entrepreneur, and a Master Gardener. Another younger sister and mother of three went on from her AS degree to earn a BA in Psychology and then to earn an MSW. She started her own Pastoral counseling service and created the Teen-Pregnancy Alliance with her Church. A younger brother with an AS degree went on to a four-year college in Florida to study Construction design before joining the Navy and working in Panama as a construction consultant. He now works as a general contractor for a construction company that specializes in scaffolding for projects involving the building and renovation of hospitals. All of them owed their starts to our local community college.

A year after receiving a summer grant at Dartmouth University from the National Endowment for the Humanities to study and research racial writing during the Civil War, I left RFCC to enroll in a PhD program in African-American Studies at a Virginia College. I wanted to continue my education, to write and publish, and to qualify for full-time teaching. After completing my dissertation on writer Dorothy West and the Harlem Renaissance, I was asked to contribute to *Notable American Women* published by Harvard University Press and to the *Encyclopedia of the Great Black Migration*. During my PhD studies, I taught both for the English Department of my College and in a special program that brought community college students from the Tidewater to my College to study composition and to utilize its classrooms, library, and facilities. The idea was to give them a taste of the atmosphere of a prominent four-year liberal arts college that they would be invited to apply to should they so desire.

With this background, why wouldn't I believe that Oceanic Community College, where I was hired, had a similar mission and commitment to its students when I joined the faculty there? I did, and I experienced the most primal kind of betrayal that I surely did not deserve. After four years of teaching and advising students, my tenure portfolio was jam-packed with my good works and achievements. Head of the Poetry Committee. Editor of *Penn*, which published student writing. Member of the Women's History Month Committee and conference presenter. Member of the Black History Month Committee and yearly presenter. Coordinator of the TYCA Writing Conference at Princeton and a presenter. Recipient of a Teaching Award from the 4 Cs National Writing Conference for innovation in teaching.

*To be, or not to be,* soon became the existential question. Not having my contract renewed for a fifth year was the go-to method for denying tenure in New Jersey. I received a letter to that effect in my mailbox in December just before the end of fall term while I was posting student grades. It couldn't have come at a worse time. Just three months earlier I had sunk all of my resources into buying my first house, in large part because in Oceanic County very few landlords will rent to tenants with a large rescue dog. Two months after the denial of contract, my father died. Were it not for the support of many good colleagues in the English Department, one of whom was the President of the faculty union, and the students who had been victimized by President Learson, who took the matter straight to the Board of Directors, I may not even have finished out the semester to complete the time left on my previous contract.

*To fight or not to fight* was an easy choice. In the long run it saved me. Because of the strength of the English Department, the faculty union did not waste any time suing Oceanic College on behalf of the three terminated candidates—one from English, one from History, and one from Math—for wrongful termination of contract based on the *arbitrary* and *capricious* actions of the College President. The students, with the assistance of the faculty, were able to retain a pro bono civil liberties attorney from a prominent law firm. They also sued Oceanic College for violations of the First Amendment and won. Ultimately, our lawsuit resulted in a settlement with substantial severance pay.

It has been a long battle, fighting my way back to where I was when I first left graduate school to fulfill my dream to be an English Professor, an academic, and a writer. I did not foresee my fate. During my first departmental interview, the English Dean assured me—for whatever reason—that "everyone gets tenure here." Four years later, at the behest of President Learson, he falsified a letter which he hid in my personnel file (without my knowledge) alleging misconduct I had certainly not committed. I found out during our lawsuit that the College Board had initially demanded that the President show cause for my termination after I addressed the Board in person with a summary of my credentials and achievements. There was no cause, so it had to be contrived. I found the Dean's complicity a stunning betrayal of the most fundamental kind. My last official act at Oceanic Community College was to make a copy of the Dean's letter and distribute it to the English faculty.

I continue to teach—tirelessly and well—but have never been hired for a tenure-track position again. There is an unwritten law of higher education: *once an adjunct, always an adjunct*. I have been afforded the occasional perks from time to time—titles and financial rewards—but they are as quickly rescinded. *Noblesse oblige* assuages guilt for some in power.

But I know better now. I know I am certainly not alone in my experience. I know that full-time, tenured faculty members are complicit with college administrations. I now question the appropriateness of tenuring anyone under these current conditions and environments. I never miss an opportunity to speak truth to power, no matter the consequences. The disregard for any person's right to gainful employment is a violation of civil and human rights.

# Academic Slavery At A Prestigious Cancer Center

## Kapil Mehta and Reeta Mehta

When a professor receives tenure, he or she is converted from an "at-will employee" (i.e., an employee whose contract can be easily ended, without the need for the employer to give a reason) to a "for cause" employee whose employment can be ended only for good reason shown at a hearing before a committee of other professors at the same institution and followed by a review from the administration. In stark contrast to the concept of academic freedom, the tenure system at one of the premier cancer centers in the country (referred to hereafter as the Texas City Cancer Center, or TCCC) has been undermined due to an arrogant "my way or no way" attitude by administration and to their never-ending greed. Things particularly started to deteriorate at this institution when a Dr. Donald Pinto took over as the fourth president in September 2011. During the four years that followed, several senior faculty members were either forced to step down or have left voluntarily to work for other institutions. An environment of low-morale, distrust, and fear of retaliation among the faculty has prevailed since then. Several senior faculty members were denied tenure renewals despite unanimous approval by the Promotion and Tenure Committee (PTC), a body of faculty members appointed by the administration's Office of Academic Affairs and charged with reviewing and recommending tenure renewals based on faculty's credentials.

Although the tenure system at Texas City Cancer Center is slightly different than other academic institutions (renewable every seven years), the decision-making process is supposed to be similar across the U.S. Indeed, a renewal process following the principles described by the American Association of University Professors (AAUP) was adopted by the TCCC (in their *Handbook of Operating Procedures*), which states that tenure renewal be considered if the applicant has retained academic credentials worthy of renewal. TCCC should have been adhering to these principles, but they were not.

Texas City Cancer Center is among the six health institutions of the University of Texas System and has been frequently referred to as the "jewel in Texas's crown." The center treats nearly 120,000 patients annually and employs more than 19,000 people, of which nearly 1,600 are faculty members. TCCC was ranked number one hospital for cancer treatment by *US News* magazine for consecutive seven years. In addition to clinical activities, TCCC offers bachelor's degrees in allied health sciences. Most of the faculty members, who are actively engaged in research, are also affiliated with the

University of Texas Graduate School of Biomedical Sciences, which offers masters and doctoral programs.

Despite unanimous approval by the PTC and strong support from the Faculty Appeal Panel, Faculty Senate, AAUP, and faculty members at large, my tenure renewal was vetoed by President Pinto without any reasons given to me. Fifteen years before my unfair dismissal, the same thing happened to my wife and she was told that nothing could be done because hers was the only complaint against this system. She kept quiet about what happened to her for fear of retaliation against me, as I was still working at TCCC. After the same thing that happened to her also happened to me, my case and another similar one were brought to the attention of the AAUP, which led a formal investigation into academic due process, shared governance, and the leadership of this institution. Based on a 37-page AAUP investigation report and unanimous approval by its members, TCCC's administration was found at fault.

Here is the background that led to the AAUP findings. I accepted my first faculty appointment at TCCC in 1983 as a research associate in the department of Clinical Immunology and Biological Therapy. In 1985, I was promoted to assistant professor with a seven-year term appointment; in 1992, I was promoted to associate professor (with a second term appointment); and in 1998, I became full professor in the Department of Experimental Therapeutics. In September 2011, two years prior to the expiration of my seven-year appointment, I submitted the required paper work to the Promotion and Tenure Committee (PTC) for review and recommendation for reappointment to a fourth term. The package included supporting letters from Dr. Gavin Howell (department chair) and Dr. Asa Wang (division head), recommending the renewal. On November 7, Dr. Howell forwarded an email message from Dr. Folger, the senior vice president for academic affairs, announcing that the PTC had unanimously approved my reappointment.

However, six months later in May 2012, Dr. Folger informed me on the phone that President Pinto had declined to accept the recommendations of the department, the division, and the PTC. I was totally shocked to learn this least expected news and immediately contacted Dr. Howell for a meeting to discuss the reasons. Dr. Howell assured me that he was unaware of the reason why Dr. Pinto overruled the PTC's recommendations. On the contrary, he expressed concern that they (Pinto and his team) might want to take over the project I had been working on for ten years, developing inhibitors against TG2, which had shown great promise for treating refractory tumors, and might have offered direction for a possible treatment for pancreatic cancer. He suggested that I meet with a member on the PTC committee from our department, who was very helpful and shared the discussion of the PTC. According to this faculty member, the PTC chair and all of the other committee members had supported my tenure renewal.

Dr. Pinto, however, rejected all the claims with false allegations (e.g., I had been awarded 3 patents related to my research between 2006 and 2011, but, according to Dr. Pinto, this was unimpressive because patents can be generated using a single figure from a publication). Immediately following this meeting, I requested another one with Dr. Folger to learn more about the reasons for Dr. Pinto's decision. Dr. Folger suggested that I resubmit my package to the PTC along with two or three letters of support from outside colleagues, a suggestion that I considered unreasonable because the PTC had already given its unanimous recommendation for renewal. My annual reviews by the department chair and division head had been positive throughout the period, and I had consistently maintained grant funding to support 30 percent of my salary, as required.

While I was still trying to find out what led to denial of my tenure renewal, the nonrenewal decision was confirmed on June 25 through a letter from Dr. Verde, the provost and executive vice president, who wrote, "In accordance with the Non-Renewal of Faculty Appointment Policy, upon the recommendation of Dr. Gavin Howell, Chair, Department of Experimental Therapeutics, and Dr. Asa Wang, Head, Division of Cancer Medicine, this letter will serve to officially notify you that your appointment as Professor with term tenure in the Department of Experimental Therapeutics, Division of Cancer Medicine, will not be renewed beyond the date of August 31, 2013. The reasons for non-renewal are that your renewal of term tenure was not approved and you will reach the maximum seven-year of term tenure appointment on August 31, 2013."

At this point, I decided to meet with Dr. Verde in July 2012. He was empathetic about the whole situation and advised me to file a grievance with the Faculty Appeal Panel (FAP), although the institution's Faculty Appeal Policy explicitly forbids it for non-renewal of tenure. He expressed that if FAP also supports the PTC's decision, it will be difficult for Dr. Pinto to deny the decision of two independent faculty panels. Accordingly, I prepared and submitted the appeal package to FAP together with new letters of support from two external colleagues.

In the meantime, Dr. Verde had left TCCC to accept a position in Utah. The newly appointed interim provost, Dr. Furtzmann informed me on October 11 that the FAP had met to review my appeal and acknowledged "lack of external funding," but did not find that "the non-renewal of appointment was arbitrary and capricious." Later, it became clear that this summary of the FAP's finding was a misrepresentation. Provost Furtzmann further wrote, "Based on my review of this matter, including current lack of expected external funding and the recommendation for nonrenewal by department chair, Professor Gavin Howell, it is my decision that the nonrenewal of your faculty appointment should be upheld. However, you have the right to appeal to the President." At this stage, I started to feel that they were giving me the run-around. Appealing back to same person (Dr.

Pinto) who over-ruled the unanimous decision of the PTC in the first place was unlikely to help.

Nevertheless, I decided to meet with the President hoping that, in educating him about my accomplishments and the promise of ongoing projects in my laboratory, I might change his mind. Before going to meet with him, I requested a copy of the FAP's written report, which was declined by Furtzmann as against "institutional policy." With the help of a senior professor, Dr. Susan Long, a former chair of the Senate Oversight Committee on Conflict Resolution, I managed to secure a copy of the panel's findings. She wrote to Dr. Furtzmann that FAP was not the appropriate process for tenure-renewal. In fact, FAP is specifically excluded from the use of appeals for non-renewal of tenure. However, it was important, per his letter, that the panel investigate and fail to find a reasonable basis for the action of non-renewal of tenure.

The FAP report sided in my favor. It stated that, "Ced Dr. Mehta has been a tenured scientist for 28 years with favorable evaluations during this period of time, with strong letters from established scientists indicating that he is well-respected among his peers." Among other positive assessments, the report cited my ongoing grant applications and their 'very favorable' scores. In the current funding environment, such reason should not warrant an ending of a career at this institution." The panelists further wrote, "The record and packet are favorably impressive. Other than a funding lull, which he is not alone in experiencing, and which could change tomorrow, we are not seeing a justifiable reason for nonrenewal." The report ended with the following recommendation: "We support the appeal and favor a 1– to 2-year grace period that, hopefully, will catalyze a rebuilding of Dr. Mehta's efforts so that he can continue his career at a stimulated level of productivity aligned with institutional goals."

On December 19, 2012, I met with the President Pinto as final step in my appeal process. Professor Sikorski, the vice-chair of the Genetics department and member of the Executive Committee of Faculty Senate, accompanied me to witness discussion during the meeting. At the end of the meeting Dr. Sikorski said, "Dr. Pinto, everything looks good in this case; what are you seeing different that everyone else is not?" The President did not give any clear answer to this. On December 31, I received a letter from Dr. Pinto announcing his final decision "to uphold the nonrenewal of appointment action."

Though I received the final letter, I was still unaware of the reasons for the nonrenewal of my appointment. On January 30, 2013, I met Dr. Folger again, to make sure that there were no negative reports/documents included in my file. Dr. Folger agreed that I had all the rights to know the reasons for nonrenewal of my position. Nevertheless, he did not have the answer as, according to him, he was not involved in the PTC or FAP process. He allowed me to review my entire dossier in his office. I could not find anything negative in the package.

In a last effort to retain me as full time faculty, my new department chair and my division head wrote a memorandum dated July 17, 2013 to the new provost requesting him to allow "a 1- to 2-year grace period for me (also recommended by the FAP)" so that I could continue my promising research, which had been recently funded by the Bayer Healthcare System and was "at the verge of receiving additional funding from the National Institutes of Health." The provost declined this request. This is how my 28-year research career ended, without knowing the reason for the injustice I endured.

The key developments in my case took place between November 2011 and June 2012 without my knowledge and were not revealed to the faculty senate, the PTC, or the FAP. We did not learn about these developments until two and a half years later when I approached the AAUP for assistance. As mentioned earlier, I was copied on the supportive recommendation of Drs. Howell and Wang for renewal of my tenure in Sept 2011, and Dr. Howell congratulated me on Nov 7 for having received PTC's unanimous vote for my tenure renewal. Two days later, Dr. Howell changed his earlier recommendation by sending an email to President Pinto and Provost Verde, copying Dr. Wang but now me. In this email, Dr. Howell recommended that the final decision on my tenure renewal be "postponed for one year to determine if Dr. Mehta could turn the situation around. . . if not, then I suggest we do not renew his term tenure in an attempt to raise the bar at this institution." He continued that "my concern stems from the institution's recommendation for renewal of term tenure for a faculty who is not able to provide the required 40 percent salary support on grants and does not have functioning research program." On June 11, 2011, Professor Howell reiterated this recommendation in an email and did not copy me. This time, writing to Dr. Verde and copying Dr. Wang, Professor Howell wrote, "I recommend that Dr. Mehta receive a nonrenewal of appointment notification in June 2012." All of this was a dirty political game behind my back and outside of the approved processes established by the institution. Even after this unethical secret was revealed, the administration of TCCC did not care to correct their wrong doings.

The administration of The Texas City Cancer Center, under the leadership of Dr. Pinto, failed to follow the institution's policy in my tenure renewal case and in how many others? A section of this policy lists possible reasons for nonrenewal, none of which pertained to my circumstances. All my annual appraisals had been favorable, and external funding from grants had consistently met the institutional requirement throughout the period of my appointment. A section of the tenure renewal procedure also stipulates that "[c]oaching or development resources may be provided to faculty before a recommendation for nonrenewal of appointment is made." None had been offered or suggested in my case. Still another section of the procedure states that "[t]he Department Chair meets with the faculty member in person to discuss the reason(s) for nonrenewal of his/her appointment." There was no such meeting, despite my repeated requests to know the reasons for my tenure nonrenewal.

Thirty-two years ago, my wife and I—both scientists—came to the United States, the land of opportunity, with big dreams. We were going to help make America great, and to do so, we left our home and loved ones in India. Despite difficult adjustments in our social and work lives, we were excited, motivated, and ready to learn. Gradually, our projects picked up speed with encouraging results. Everyday was exciting with new findings that generated new challenges. Our research led to the development of a new drug for successful treatment of fungal infections in patients. It was a win-win situation for all: scientists, patients, institutions, and the company involved in the pharmaceutical production. We got research grants, popularity, and royalties for a few years. My wife was a mere six months away from receiving half a million dollars in royalty money from a previous project that would fund the research she was doing. In the middle of her contract year, she was told that her salary could not be supported anymore. Her boss advised her to talk to the head of the department. During that meeting she was told not to worry. Then she was sent to the division head; he then sent her back to her boss with the same words of assurance. She met with other administrators. They gave her the run around just like they would eventually give me. Just a few months before they let her go, these same people had nothing but compliments for her work during her annual evaluation. Nobody helped to save her hard-earned career. She suffered with terrible depression and health issues after that and relived all of it when the same thing happened to me.

Based on the recommendations of the Investigating Committee and failure of TCCC administrators to remedy their wrong doings, AAUP members, at their annual meeting in the summer of 2015, voted unanimously to impose censorship on the TCCC administration. But what happened first to my wife and then to me is troubling in a larger sense. Educators are already concerned about the upcoming generations' lack of interest in science. Others are worried about the status of the U.S. in the scientific research arena. With administrators who care only for their high-figure salaries and with surrounding themselves with people who will keep them in power and eliminate anyone who gets in their way, we should be very concerned about the future of this country in terms of remaining competitive in the sciences and other fields. Thus far these unfair dismissals have been viewed as individual anomalies involving faculty who are suspected guilty of some shortfall even though none could be proven. The AAUP's report after my unfair dismissal has begun to suggest that poor leadership of academic institutions could be a national security issue in terms of risking our competitive edge in knowledge production. By the time we admit the larger pattern, it could be too late. The administration caste will have gotten rich off of the unethical hirings and firings they orchestrate, like fascist dictators, to keep themselves in power and to keep word of their incompetency and greed from spreading, but they will have bankrupted the ethics and intellect of our country.

# Outside The Outside

*Karen Salyer McElmurray*

Just five years ago, I survived my own ending. Came through treatment following a diagnosis of stage three colorectal cancer. This, in itself, is a familiar story. *Woman faced with major illness.* Chemo. Surgeries. Lymph nodes, potential cell migrations. But the ending? *The furthest part or point of something.* My synapses came alive.

*A nerve ending.* The point at which I began to reevaluate my life.

I had the job writers most want. Full time faculty member in an MFA Program, complete with editorship for a nationally recognized literary magazine, a reading series, and mentorship for bright, young writers finding their voices. But I knew that I needed an environment that nurtures the creative—and I had not found that in my workplace. I wanted community. Respectful and non-hierarchical thinking. I wanted to begin again.

\* \* \*

Where I grew up, education itself can seem like a strange and foreign country. In the Eastern Kentucky I grew up in, a lot of people quit school as soon as they can or as soon as circumstances make that necessary. High school boys quit to buy coal rigs. Girls quit school, becoming mothers. I almost quit school myself when I became pregnant at fifteen, with a son I relinquished to social services and a state-supported adoption. I was poor, married to a boy one year older than me who worked at a grocery store and stole steaks and rolls of cookie dough for our suppers. Once we divorced, my own jobs over the next few years were fast food, maid, checker at a convenience store.

My odds weren't good for higher education. Lots of fine people, so my father told me once I left home, never went on to college. He encouraged me to study shorthand and typing. Nor were the female role models in my family very encouraging. Only one woman, an aunt by marriage on my father's side, went to college at all, and she was an elementary school teacher. My aunts on my mother's side all finished high school, but then they settled in to becoming wives, then into depression and divorce and fundamentalist religion, one of the main ways I grew up seeing women in my mountain culture having a voice at all—a voice raised in praise of God the Father.

Following my son's relinquishment, I worked as cook, secretary, landscaper, sporting towel folder, greenhouse worker—but my father, a high school math teacher, had early on instilled in me the hunger for a college education, even if he didn't necessarily encourage me to get one for myself and didn't support my efforts in that direction. So I attended night school, community college, applied for every grant I could get my hands on so I could finish my undergraduate degree at Berea College, where I was a weaver and a teaching assistant as I studied literature and philosophy. After graduation, I found myself employed at a child care center. On the phone one day a friend from college asked me just what I thought I was doing, anyway, surrounded by thirty children and oceans of spilled milk. Soon I applied for more schooling. I graduated from an MFA program, an MA program, a doctoral program. I became Visiting Assistant Professor, Writer in Residence, Assistant Professor, twice. Associate Professor, Professor-on-her-way-to-the-stars. I wrote and published books. Papers mounted on my kitchen table. Over the years I have taught everything from World Literature to the Literature of Railroads. I have traveled between genres, crossed more state lines than I can count. Climbed an invisible rope that burned my hands. I became, as one of my best friends has told me, driven.

In the midst of that drivenness? Memory. Sometimes, the sadness of the women I've left behind. The aunt who ran off to be a go-go dancer, leaving behind the daughter who passed from family to family. The cousin who almost went to college, but ended up weighing in at almost four hundred pounds before she died, her lungs and heart and kidneys and self, given out. The aunt who almost never leaves her trailer and can see the grave of her son in the family cemetery on the hill beyond her kitchen window. And my own mother. For almost forty years she told me she wished she'd done something with herself after high school. *Gone on to business school. Learned to be a secretary or a nurse or a kindergarten teacher.* Used to be, when I'd go to visit her, she'd have the Kentucky Driver's License Manual sitting out on the coffee table. She'd have underlined key phrases about parallel parking, caution signs and turn signals. She'd wave the manual in my face. *I just might learn how to drive,* she'd say. *I ought to.*

In this tableau of women's lives, the memory I return to most often is my Aunt Della. Aunt Della owned a restaurant and diner called The Black Cat. She fixed brakes, changed oil, fried eggs, paid the bills. It was the 1950's and women didn't do jobs like that much. My Aunt, they say, was odd-turned. *Contrary.* I've written stories about her, her big hands, black-streaked and strong from hard work. I imagine her reaching down into some vat of soaking spark plugs, some geography of wires and hoses. What message did the faulty hearts of engines send back? Della, I used to think, was the one I most wanted to be.

* * *

The time I first thought about leaving my job I was in a crowd celebrating thesis defenses and pending graduations, standing next to a woman I'll call Ava. She was a second-year student in nonfiction. Ava had traveled, spent a lot of time in Peru, and she'd traveled emotional realms, too. She was writing about drug addiction and alcoholism, about, at last, her ability to find love. I was her thesis advisor, but I had been ill and was planning an exit for a while to get myself on my feet again. I was worried about where I'd leave her and her work.

Ava and I were, as we sometimes joked, free range lyricists. We wrote non-linearly, for the most part. We were both interested in intimate writing, writing that appealed to a private self, an interior self. We were both a little older, her as an MFA student, me as a woman getting established in a career. And we'd both experienced edges. Me with my cancer, and Ava, too, who had just experienced a series of miscarriages and then a long, difficult pregnancy. Since that pregnancy, there'd been concern about the impact on her teaching assistantship. The missed classes. The incompletes on her record.

How pretty Ava looked with her newly cut hair, an asymmetrical style that echoed the question she was trying to ask. I sipped my wine and listened. *Could her thesis be part poems and part memoir?* She was struggling to fill pages, to find the time to write. She'd finally had the baby, a beautiful boy I'd gotten to hold while he was swaddled, fresh from the hospital.

Before I could answer, the boy-writers began to gather at the bar. Mark. Tom. Randy. And the director of the writing program. Glass of Jack Daniels in hand, two sheets to the wind like the rest of us.

My writing program's director was a poet in a school that, like much of increasingly corporatized academia, doesn't know what to do with its artists. He's a good enough poet, married to a school administrator, with no children of his own. He wants awards, publications, for himself and his program. He was impatient with Ava, the miscarriages that took her out of the classroom, the pregnancy that left her bed ridden, the baby that had to come first. He wanted her to finish up, pronto, move on out, make room for those more reliable and good for the program than herself.

I drank white wine while the director finished his Jack Daniels, his plump cheeks flushed. Anyone here pregnant, he asked. He studied the five of us, his gaze moving across Ava. Don't get pregnant, now, he said as he wagged a finger at the boys.

I could almost hear it. Ava's missed classes, clinking in his brain like ice in a glass. The sound of a joke that wasn't one. The quiet, after.

\* \* \*

I have thought again and again about my Aunt Della and her cars over my years as a teacher of creative writing. I can still see her as she came back from the garage and sat at one of the diner booths, after she'd worked out in the garage. By then, her marriage to my Uncle Russell was on the rocks, and he worked the kitchen while she managed the garage. They didn't talk much, hadn't for a good long while, and he ended up, by the time I was nine, dying in the front seat of his Chevy Impala, radio and heater on, after Della locked him out after he'd laid out all night, drinking and playing poker.

Before that tragedy is what I remember her most. Her at the table, me underneath that table, staring up at the chewing gum somebody had left behind and listening to Bob Willis and the Texas Playboys on the jukebox. *Where did you come from, where did you go? Where did you come from, Cotton Eyed Joe?* Later on, she'd order me a grilled cheese with dill pickles and I'd sit with her and study her hands. Those freckle-backed, leathery brown hands. How she held her coffee mug with one hand and cradled a cigarette in the other. *You're a pretty little thing, ain't you,* she'd say. And she'd talk about her daughter, Rita, who'd moved off up north and become a big lawyer.

It is certain that part of my own ambition to leave Kentucky and myself become something big dates from those times. Della's hands, with their black-edged nails, thick and misshapen with work, were hands that knew how to do things. All these years later, in creative writing classes, that *knowing* is what I have wanted. Intuitive. Close to the bone. That kind of knowledge. In my workshops, I ask writers to talk about "the heart" of a work at hand. Its intentions. What it is about, and why, and then how, via craft, can that heart be furthered. A memory of hands. The heart. Heartwood, that botany term for the part of the wood that is hardest of all.

\* \* \*

It took me over five years to make my decision to leave my academic position. Two years of radiation and chemo and two major surgeries. Three years of recovery. The long while after that to agonize over what I could afford, what I couldn't, in ways practical and philosophical. Would I be able to find enough work on my own, out of the system, to be self-sufficient? I'd been living at a distance from my husband for over six years, but would I be turning my life over to him if I left my job? *Never depend on anyone,* my program director said, when I tried to discuss my options. *That's what my wife has always taught me!* I see myself at other strategic moments during that time of confusion and uncertainty. We were sitting in a conference room, the director and I. I'd challenged him on whether we should award a fiction prize to a student when I knew the piece from a class in nonfiction. *Is that ethical,* I asked. *Do you really care about being ethical,* he asked, his voice incredulous, belittling of my question. The trouble is I cared too much. I was beset by every angle of my decision, every outcome and option. I felt angry, voiceless.

It would be far too easy to let this short essay devolve into a list of grievances and complaints. To let it devolve into more scenes from my previous position, ones in which I found myself and the women I worked with devalued, patronized or criticized. And along with that dynamic, my mounting frustration that what we were teaching was not writing itself, really, but the pursuit of the teaching position, the publisher, the rank and file. Listing grievances is not my intention here, and it is not useful for that larger subject, the one most important to me these days: the making of art via the written word. Other writers I've met have faced equally hard choices where that subject is concerned.

One woman wrote me her story of leaving a similar job, her realization that she had to leave behind toxicity in order to remember who she was, a writer first and foremost. And another friend, a poet who drove me to the airport a few weeks back and also left tenure. He said this. "I have realized that I wanted to work in order to support my poetry—not write to support the job. I seldom wrote any more. Instead I spent my time lobbying for the next grant, for lines on my vita, for opportunities that would propel me forward. I had, in the end, forgotten what *forward* meant. I came to realize, finally, that forward meant family, happiness, a balanced life—all of which are necessary to my writing life."

The truth is, I am not always certain what exactly is necessary for my life as a writer. If I drive the miles all the way back to that little town in Eastern Kentucky where I come from, I feel like a stranger in a strange country, one in which I am, these days, a foreigner. No one reads much, and when I see them, they seldom mention my life as *a writer*, that weird anomaly, with its undertones of English class and grammar, its high-minded sound, its intimidation factor. *A writer. Just who do you think you are, anyway?* The truth is I have also felt like a stranger in the halls of academe, its offices and faculty meetings, its politics and intrigues. *Just who was I, anyway?* The first woman in my family to go to college. As the nine years of my job went by, I feared becoming the director himself. Or the professor down the hall who never writes, but must, for merit pay, for end-of-year reports, for research credit. I was a writer of poetic prose, of emotions and memories and light, a writer who didn't quite know what to make of the colleagues who disdained writing personal stories, who disparaged memoir as a lesser form. *Just who do I think I am?*

\* \* \*

Where I used to think I came alive most fully was in the company of other women. Women friends. Other women writers and artists. We all inhabited, I believed, that wild zone Elaine Showalter describes in her essay, "Feminist Criticism in the Wilderness." "We can think of the 'wild zone' of women's culture spatially, experientially, or metaphysically," Showalter says. "Spatially it stands for an area which is literally no-man's-land, a place forbidden to men. . . Experientially it stands for the aspects of the female life-style which are outside of and unlike those of men; again, there is a corresponding zone of male experience alien to women. But if we think of the wild zone metaphysically, or in terms of consciousness, it has no corresponding male space since all of male consciousness is within the circle of the dominant structure and thus accessible to or structured by language. In this sense, the 'wild' is always imaginary." But I was forever frustrated that the women I worked with in the academy often didn't belong in that female space, either. *Butter them up more*, said one of my female colleagues. This was advice I could not tolerate.

The truth is I clung to the idea of my job longer than I clung to the job itself. The money, of course. I'd been poor much of my life before coming to academia. Had lived on everything from food stamps to jobs cleaning houses. Security was a very hard thing to surrender. Still this was not what haunted me the most. As Patricia Foster, in her essay, "The Intelligent Heart," writing deeply about the self is "the source, the goods, the first principle from which everything else is made." I'd believed that by teaching creative writing I was teaching a way of thinking, a way of diving deeper, understanding the world and one's place in that world, be it socially or politically or spiritually. In the growing discussions of enrollment numbers and national rankings, I grew more and more unsure of what I believed or why.

I want to return for a moment to that night of the cocktail party and my student. Her difficult pregnancies. The sad warnings of the director about pregnancy. *Is anybody pregnant? Don't get pregnant!* What I think, in the end, is that all writers are pregnant. We're pregnant with memories that must be told. With the summoned memories of hands and coffee cups, of the sad, lined faces of loved ones we will lose to time, as surely as they have lost loved ones, as surely as we will all learn what it is we can hold onto, what we cannot. As Patricia Hampl says in "Memory and Imagination," "our capacity to move forward as developing beings rests on a healthy relation with the past." What we all must do, I realized in those last weeks before I resigned my position, is tell our stories—nonfiction or poetry, novels or stories. We're pregnant with these stories, stories fecund and rich, ripe and necessary.

* * *

I was an outsider. I belonged outside the outside.

It was like this I often tried to teach words.

I reached outside for them, and inside too. Outside myself and my neat, clean desk. Back to the garage where Della worked. Down into the engine of some old Dodge Dart, its engine block cracked and spewing steam. I reached down and patched holes with stove cement and grease. I reached down inside and got hold.

I reached inside unsavory places. The lungs, the gut, the unwilling heart. Tell me, I said to the words and those who wrote them. Tell me truths, even if they are not pretty, even if they taste bitter and they hurt.

Open, I told the words and their makers. Come alive.

\* \* \*

These days, I'm living with my partner and doing my best to work for myself in an uncertain job market. I'm teaching in new ways. Classes at a women's shelter, this last summer. Teaching for conferences, picking up creative writing classes at schools nearby, trying to summon my own words with clarity I haven't had for a long while. Twice each year, I teach at low-residency writing programs, where the students are writing while they conduct other, busy professional lives. I like this work, and I like these voices. These students with full lives who are trying to make room for creativity.

Recently, when I was teaching at one of the residencies, I was up in my room for the night. As I lay there, lights off, trying to relax before the following day of teaching and talking about the writing life, the world was so alive I couldn't sleep. It was late, but downstairs, I heard cheering, on screen and off. There was a football game on television. I imagined hurrahs from the bar down the street, shouting from the lawn. There was a lot to shout about. Next day, the score announced would be 42 to 14, Alabama over Notre Dame. But that night as I lay there, what I was thinking about was the nature of competition itself. Words from game world. *Goals. Yards earned. Points.* Those words circled in my head with similar words and phrases from the previous days at the residency. *Earned a position. Books snatched up by so and so. Works meets its goal.*

What is the goal of the writing life?

For years, my own goal has been success as much as anything. I've lobbied for jobs, grants, fellowships, agents, publishers, publications. And those, I still know, are the necessary tools of the trade, the reality of the writing business. I want those tools of the trade as much as anyone else.

Since my illness, there are parts of the game I no longer want. The inner critic's rules. *She thinks we're more talented than she is.* Or I walk into a big writer's conference with my husband and he says, "you can feel the force of the egos in the air," and I want to shrug this off. But I feel it as much as he does. Another friend says this. *I'm tired of not being invited to the table in the writing world. When am I going to get there?* I want to take the high road, tell her that there is only one table, artistry, and that we all eat there. But secretly, I have the same fears. The same resentments concerning who is publishing where, how many books so and so has, how fast those books were written and what job at which place those books have earned her.

Lewis Hyde quotes Joseph Conrad in *The Gift: Creativity and the Artist in the Modern World.* "The artist appeals... to that in us which is a gift and not an acquisition--and, therefore, more permanently enduring. Art speaks to our capacity for delight and wonder, to the sense of mystery surrounding our lives; to our sense of pity, and beauty, and pain; to the latent feeling of fellowship with all creation—to the subtle but invincible conviction of solidarity that knits together the loneliness of innumerable hearts, to the solidarity... which binds together all humanity—the dead to the living and the living to the unborn.'"

On the night of the big game, I found myself thinking, as I often do, about my Aunt Della. About her hands. Hands, I say, that knew how to do things. Set a spark plug gap just right. Set an engine purring down the road. How I want to take these words I write, these words I teach, and set them purring like the engines she knew like the backs of her own hands. That night I lay sleepless a long time, watching the shadows of branches move across the window blinds and listening to the voices downstairs. I wanted to know how to go there and sit and wait for the real words to find their way.

# Why I Quit My Teaching Career in Texas, and Why I Understand If You Do the Same

## *Duana Welch*

Oil, cotton, the fine grit that coats the teeth of happy West Texans: that January, those scents greeted me like long-lost friends as I returned to a place inhabited by my relatives before there was an Alamo to remember. They took me back to a happy childhood of fishing with one grandfather and feeding the cattle with the other, eating cookies baked by an indulgent great-grandma, celebrating July 4$^{th}$ with an entire community, and, at age seven, biking by myself all over a town where everyone knew everyone else—a town largely unacknowledged by the larger world, except by those who recalled its one stoplight as they barreled through Post towards Lubbock.

I was there for my last remaining grandparent's funeral; I was there to recall the good times. I was there from a long distance away, politically and geographically: Eugene, Oregon.

My parents, who grew up and married one another in Post, moved my brother and me to San Antonio when we were toddlers. By age 21, I left the state for graduate school at the University of Florida, followed by a tenure-track professorship at Cal State Fullerton's psychology department. Eventually, due to a family crisis, I moved to Austin with my daughter—vowing that this time, I wouldn't be leaving again.

How wrong I was.

At the time, I meant it. There were so many reasons to stay. My mom, dad, brother, and other beloveds were in easy distance of Austin. Life was good; I had remarried a man who had spent 30 years there, and we had a community we loved. The school system our kids attended was remarkably free of the thought-suppression Texas' textbooks are known for. And I had the best job of my life.

A lot of part-time faculty are dissatisfied with their careers and the way they're treated, and who can blame them? Increasingly, institutions unfairly rely on adjuncts, all the while underpaying them, offering an unstable career with few perks and even less respect. Often, the percentage of adjuncts is 70% or greater, yet they are not given a voice in governing their departments or institutions, and their positions are continually tenuous rather than tenured.

Yet I loved adjunct teaching at Austin Community College. Not only was I fairly compensated for my work, on a pay scale that was public and which rewarded my degrees, career experience, and years of service to ACC, but I was respected. Adjuncts had as much chance as anyone to receive awards and acknowledgements, and I was given a NISOD award and honored at the first-ever ACC faculty awards banquet. I had the ear of my colleagues, the Chair, the Dean, and the President whenever I wanted to speak with them. I was a voting member of the faculty—not relegated to a separate and unequal group, but included with full-timers who were my full peers. I served on committees on a voluntary basis, chaired one, and was paid for all time spent serving the greater institution. When I attended events intended to boost involvement in the institution, or when I applied for retreats and programs designed to enhance collegiality and teaching skills, I was treated as an equal and as if my presence were desirable. I had job security: although nobody, full- or part-time at ACC had tenure, part-timers were eligible for an ongoing appointment. Within a couple of years, I was at highest priority to teach the three course sections I most wanted, semester after semester.

And the students—I loved them. I admired their dedication to learning, despite life circumstances that often made attendance and scholarship difficult. I respected their work ethic, and I was often humbled by the fact that so many of them were spread thin with commitments to full-time work, raising young children, and achieving at school. For instance, I was honored to know a student who stayed in college despite raising five young children under the age of five—including her siblings' kids—, although the student was under drinking age herself. I met with heroism, mundane to sublime, every day. I felt deeply fortunate to be there.

In 2014, I put Austin Community College in my will, and told every class I taught, "I am never going to retire. Someday, I will die while teaching, and you'll have to carry me out."

The implication was that I would be at ACC forever, dying of old age at the lectern.

The hitch was my unwillingness to die from gunshot.

At the 2014 national mid-term elections, Oregon had a 78% voter turnout. Texas had 9%. Throw in active voter-suppression, a downtrodden progressive electorate that feels defeated before they even leave the house, and gerrymandering aimed at keeping the far-right in perpetual power, and it's little wonder that Texas was one of very few states to go farther right that year. At a time when the Tea Party was being rooted out, Texas—or rather, a tiny slice of voters—embraced it.

So, in early 2015, while Oregon's leadership passed laws to reduce tuition at community colleges and expand access to higher education, Texas' new leaders stated that priority #1 was getting guns into college classrooms by not only permitting concealed carry on campuses—but disallowing public institutions to decide that they would prefer to be exempt. (Private universities were able to determine whether they would allow campus carry, and as of this writing, all of those that have made a decision have decided against it.) Although polls indicated that most Texans of both parties were opposed, Texas governor Greg Abbott swore he would sign the bill into law as soon as it crossed his desk.

It wasn't the first time Texas representatives had tried to pass campus carry; it had been proposed in the prior two legislative sessions. Those efforts failed because the legislation was not as far-right and the votes to pass the bill were lacking. But this time, the Tea Party was in charge—and they decided to change the rules governing how laws come about. Whereas it had formerly taken a two-thirds majority to pass legislation in the Texas House and Senate, the new legislators made new rules that henceforth, it would only take half. That way, they would have the votes needed to push through the new gun laws.

For the 2011 and 2013 legislative sessions, I had called lawmakers, asking them not to pass this law. In the 2015 session, I did more than that. I asked many of my students in anonymous feedback to indicate their degree of support for campus carry. Ninety percent were opposed, many because they were minorities and felt that this would target them, or because they were young women who feared reprisal from hotheaded ex-boyfriends, or because they felt less safe with more guns around, or because they wondered whether the free exchange of ideas core to collegiate learning could really happen when there was such a powerfully implied "or else" between faculty and students.

I spoke with colleagues, too. At a teaching retreat in Bandera, Texas that March, I attended a forum for Safety In The Classroom. Before revealing my own plans to exit the state should the measure pass, I asked, "What do you plan to do to remain safe when the campus carry bill becomes law?" I was stunned by the reaction: almost 60% said that they planned to stop professing in Texas within the ensuing three to five years, either by retiring, moving to another state to continue teaching, or changing their profession to focus on consulting and other non-professorial activities.

Afterwards, I called and wrote to every Texas Senator and most members of its House, detailing what I had learned. I also spoke in the Senate and faced the elected officials who would be putting my and my students' lives on the line.

When you speak to Texas' legislators, you are given a brief time in a public forum to present your case. As I waited my turn, I heard many arguments against, and a few in favor. Most people focused on whether they believed more guns would make them safer. My argument was different. What if you pass campus carry into law, and your professors leave? What if Texas loses its academic credibility and its ability to attract the best faculty and students? What if the classrooms you have a right to carry into are unstaffed?

I said my piece. But I could see the Senators' resolve that they were simply going through the motions, ticking off the boxes until they could vote the way they, and presumably the NRA, had predetermined.

Seeing their determination made me reexamine my position. Was I really afraid of being murdered by a student? No. In truth, I have a long history of positive and warm relationships with my students, and even after I have moved, that has continued. I've written more letters of recommendation for them this year than in most prior years, and they frequently write or call: "I graduated!" "I got the promotion!" "I'm getting married!" Or, tragically, "Our baby died. Can you please call now?"

But part of me—maybe the part that is a sixth-generation Texan—stubbornly dug in and refused to teach under the new law. I could not escape the suspicion that my students' reactions were correct. My reading of social science leads me to think my minority students are at greater risk of being on the receiving end of gun violence, as are my young female students. And we are all at greater risk of an end to the flow of ideas and mutual regard that mark intellectual freedom in the college environment. I had left a six-figure career in public relations to return to professing, taking an 80% pay cut in the process, and I had done it to have a nurturing relationship with my students. This law, I feel, damages that relationship, inherently placing a burden of mistrust on all in a classroom, even if nobody ever pulls a gun.

Leaving wasn't easy, and in many ways, my family's thought process and mine mirrored common reactions to any major loss. Denial, anger, bargaining, depression, and acceptance all made their appearance several times, in a confusing and painful jumble. I feared uprooting my family. We had identified the Pacific Northwest as our likely destination. What if any one of us couldn't make the adjustment—to the seven full months of rain, to the long dark nights, to the loss of old friends, to new ways and a loss of the familiar and comfortable? What if I couldn't stand leaving my mother again, or she needed me and I wasn't there? What if my teenage daughter never forgave me for moving her away from what we had all assumed was her home until college? You may laugh, but I have met many adults in their forties who are still angry at their parents for that very thing. What if my husband, who had spent a lifetime improving our Austin neighborhood and who was highly regarded as a career for lions, tigers, and—yes—bears, felt he had given up too much by moving? What if they all resented me and ultimately felt that I should have put up with the new law and gone in to teach anyway? What if I never found another teaching job? And, after three decades on both sides of the desk, I wondered: Who will I be without a classroom?

These worries kept me up at night. They woke me from deep slumber. Because of these fears, and a need to do what fit best for everyone, we at first discussed the possibility of my focusing on my publishing business, speaking engagements, and authorship, while remaining in Texas. But Texas had also passed laws allowing open carry in public. Were we really going to allow our daughter to bag groceries where people were packing heat? Were we going to send her to UT Austin, her first choice, where other students were armed? Were we going to continue endorsing Texas' bad laws by remaining in the state when we had options to go elsewhere?

No. We weren't.

On July 1, 2015, we arrived in Eugene, Oregon. Only one of us, my husband Vic, had ever seen it in person before, for four days the preceding May. But by moving day, we were all on board; a good thing since our Austin house had sold quickly and there was no home to return to.

Here's what happened next: life unfolded beautifully, in ways we could not have expected. Yes, we had losses. But there are many things we've found. We found out we had cousins here. We found a like-minded community of friends here. Vic found meaningful work, with people as well as animals. Our daughter found that she liked her new high school and her new youth group. We all found that we can embrace stormy weather and, like Oregon natives, live without umbrellas.

And I didn't have to find out who I am without a classroom. My goal of teaching at Lane Community College has not yet been realized, mainly because LCC is appropriately devoted to filling classes for their existing adjuncts, many of whom have been there for decades. But I've been teaching since January, first to two community classes of adults who want to apply relationship science to their lives, and now at the high school for the performing arts, where I conduct a weekly seminar on healthy relationships from a scientific basis. Plus, my longtime relationship coaching practice has its first-ever downtown office, where it is attracting an enthusiastic base of adults who want to use factual information to make informed choices in their personal lives.

Ultimately, there are students everywhere, and I didn't have to remain in a situation I found untenable to continue being involved in education. I don't blame faculty and families who are living under the domain of these laws, just as I hope they don't blame me for deciding not to. People have many life circumstances and reasons for making big decisions, and not everyone can pick up and move. Others may decide that remaining in place and protesting the laws in an ongoing way is the better battle; I honor and respect that, and in a way, I agree with them. I had protested for as long as I was willing, but there is tension within me as I face the certain knowledge that if all educators truly abandon my home state, the implications will be negative and far-reaching for millions of people.

When I was back in West Texas for my grandfather's funeral, it was clear that some in Post had heard about my move, and why I had made it. A judge who had been my granddaddy's friend asked me, "What do you think of this part of the world?" He seemed surprised when I replied, "I love it. I love the wide-open spaces and the wildness of the land and the friendliness of the people."

I was telling the truth. I don't appreciate the turn Texas politics has taken over a period of decades, but I love the land and the people. Now, though, I'm loving new people in a new land, where someday, the scent of moss, fir trees, and musty dampness will tug at my heart in sweet memory.

# About the Authors

**Robert E. Brown** is a professor in the Communications Department of at Salem State University in Massachusetts. From 1990 to 2013, he was also an adjunct professor of Communications at the Harvard Extension School. Dr. Brown's *The Public Relations of Everything* (Routledge 2014) rethinks the concept of public relations as a humanities-based discipline. Brown is the author of more than 100 essays, articles, poems, op-eds, a book, a poetry "chapbook," and the co-author of a book of poetry translations. His essays on culture and politics also appear occasionally in the *Boston Globe* and other newspapers, including the *Salem News*. Brown was a Contributing Writer for the social science magazine *Human Behavior*.

**Kathleen Davies** (PhD, Indiana University, 1991) is a retired English and Women's Studies professor, who has published creative nonfiction in *South Loop Review*, *AGS Quarterly*, *Ray's Road Review*, and *Imitation Fruit*. She is currently finishing a book-length memoir, entitled *Sacred Groves: How a Victorian Cemetery Saved a Professor's Soul*. After being denied tenure, she worked as an adjunct until finding a home at Ohio University-Chillicothe, where she taught for many years as an untenured assistant professor. She lives in Columbus, Ohio, with her fiancé and their Welsh Corgi, Robby.

**Madeline Grey** holds a PhD and an MFA, and works at Knight & Grey Publishing, as well as elsewhere, as an editor, technical writer, and graphic designer. She manages KarmaKindler.com and the Wordwrite Book Awards.

**Nancy McCabe**'s creative nonfiction has appeared in numerous publications, including *Fourth Genre*, *Prairie Schooner*, *Newsweek*, and *Gulf Coast*. It has also won a Pushcart and made notable lists six times in Houghton-Mifflin Best American anthologies. Most recently, her essays have been anthologized in *Every Father's Daughter: 24 Women Writers Remember their Fathers*; *Oh Baby! True Stories about Conception, Adoption, Surrogacy, Pregnancy, Labor, and Love*; *A Pink Suitcase: 22 Tales of Women's Travel*; and *The Nancy Drew Anthology*. Her books include a novel, *Following Disasters*, an essay collection,

*After the Flashlight Man: A Memoir of Awakening*, and three memoirs, *Meeting Sophie: A Memoir of Adoption*; *Crossing the Blue Willow Bridge: A Journey to My Daughter's Birthplace in China*; and *From Little Houses to Little Women: Revisiting a Literary Childhood*. She directs the writing program at the University of Pittsburgh at Bradford and teaches in the low-residency MFA program at Spalding University.

**Karen Salyer McElmurray** 's *Surrendered Child: A Birth Mother's Journey*, was an AWP Award Winner for Creative Nonfiction. Her novels are *The Motel of the Stars*, Editor's Pick by Oxford American, and *Strange Birds in the Tree of Heaven*, winner of the Chaffin Award for Appalachian Writing. Other stories and essays have appeared in *Iron Horse, Kenyon Review, Alaska Quarterly Review*, and *Riverteeth*, and in the anthologies *An Angle of Vision; To Tell the Truth; Fearless Confessions; Listen Here; Dirt; Family Trouble;* and *Red Holler*. Her writing has been supported by grants from the National Endowment for the Arts, the North Carolina Arts Council, and the Kentucky Foundation for Women. Recent essays have been named Notable in Best American Essays 2016, as well as winner of the Annie Dillard Award for Nonfiction and The New Southerner Creative Nonfiction Prize. She teaches creative writing at Gettysburg College and in the Low Residency MFA Program at West Virginia Wesleyan College.

**Kapil and Reeta Mehta** are both former research scientists at the University of Texas Cancer Center. Professor Kapil Mehta is in the field of experimental therapeutics and currently serves on the Board of Directors for Molecular Quest, a biotech company in India, and as Scientific Advisor for Lifecare Innovations. Reeta Mehta is in the field of microbial biochemistry and bio-immunotherapy.

**Edward Rafferty** is a teacher and writer living in Concord, MA. He received his M.A. (1992) and Ph.D (1999) from Brown University in History. He has taught at the University of Rhode Island, Simmons College, and Boston University, and worked at museums and in digital publishing since leaving graduate school. His first book, *Apostle of Human Progress: Lester Frank Ward and American Political Thought, 1841-1913*, appeared at the end of 2003. In addition, he has written numerous essays and reviews in historical publications dealing with 19th and 20th century intellectual history, the history of American reform, and American environmentalism. He currently teaches at

Concord Academy and is working on essays about environmental history and pieces of creative non-fiction.

**Michaela Valentine** is the pen name of an earnest educator located east of the Taconic Mountains.

**Duana C. Welch**, Ph.D. is the author of *Love Factually: 10 Proven Steps from I Wish to I Do*. She writes for *Psychology Today* and her blog, *LoveScience,* coaches clients globally who want more love in their lives, and teaches men and women how to use social science to find and keep the right partner. She lives in Eugene, Oregon, with her husband, daughter, and assorted critters, and when she's not writing or teaching, she enjoys hiking, sampling dark chocolate, and embracing her inner nerd.

Essays by **J.W. Young** have been anthologized by Dzanc Books and Random House. Her work has appeared in various literary journals and magazines. She teaches literature and composition in Georgia where she lives with her husband and their three devilish children. You can connect with her on Facebook and Twitter.

# Further Reading

Lennard J. Davis. "Beyond Tenure," *Chronicle of Higher Education* (April 18, 1998).

Annunziata, Maria. 2004. "Dead Professor Walking." *The Chronicle Career Network*, 31 August. http://chronicle.com/jobs/2004/08/20040831 Ole.html.

Baron, Dennis. 2003. "Life After Tenure." *The Chronicle of Higher Education*, 23 July, C3-4.

Davis, Lennard J. 1998."Beyond Tenure: A Tortuous Journey through Academe." *The Chronicle of Higher Education*, 17 April, B6-7.

Jasper, James M. 2001a "Institutions Are Not Your Friends." The Chronicle of Higher Education Career Network, 31 August. http://chronicle.com/jobs/2001/08/ 2001083102c.htm.

-----. 2001b "Moving On After You Are Denied Tenure." The Chronicle of Higher Education Career Network, 1 June. http://chronicle.com/jobs/2001/06/ 2001060103c.htm.

-----. 2001c. "What It's Like To Bc Denied Tenure." The Chronicle of Higher Education Career Network, 6 April. http://chronicle.com/jobs/2001/04/2001040602c.hm1.

Kolodny, Annette. *Failing the Future: A Dean Looks at Higher Education in the Twenty-first Century*. Durham: Duke University Press, 1998.

McKelly, James C. 1997. "The Naked and the Dead: Dispatches from the Tenure Wars." *In Profession* 1997. New York: MLA.

Shapiro, Judith. 2001. "Winning Tenure, Losing the Thrill." *The Chronicle Review*. The Chronicle of Higher Education, 16 November, B7-B9.

Wilson, Robin. 1998."'It's Like You Have Leprosy': The Year After Losing a Tenure Bid." The Chronicle of Higher Education, 6 March, A12-13.

Stivale, Charles J. "Tenure and its Denial: Facing the Winter Years and Beyond" *College Literature* 33.2 (spring 2006): 70-83.

Westheimer, Joel "Anti-Unionism and Anti-Intellectualism" *Social Text* 2002: 47-64.

www.ingramcontent.com/pod-product-compliance
Lightning Source LLC
Chambersburg PA
CBHW071516080526
44588CB00011B/1447